MICHELLE WINCHESTER

# The Beginner's Guide to SEWING FOR COSTUMING

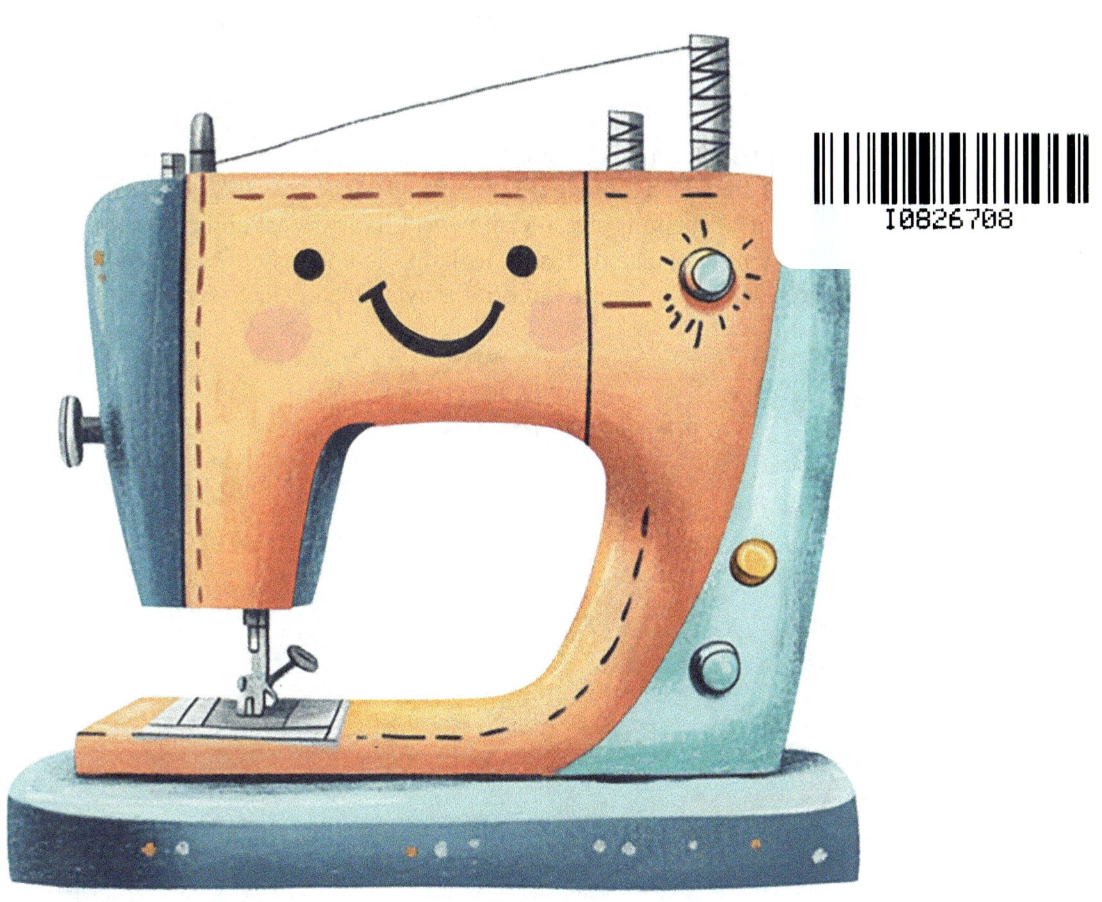

Library Tales Publishing
www.LibraryTalesPublishing.com
www.Facebook.com/LibraryTalesPublishing

Published in New York, New York.



For general information on our other products and services, please contact our Customer Care Department at 1-800-754-5016, or fax 917-463-0892.
For technical support, please visit www.LibraryTalesPublishing.com
Library Tales Publishing also publishes its books in a variety of electronic formats. Every content that appears in print is available in electronic books.

ISBN
9798894410265
Printed in the United States of America

# TABLE OF CONTENTS

## Dedicated to:

**Aurora**, who thinks I'm magic.

**Nick**, always ready to bug out.

**Monica**, who refuses to take "no" for an answer.

**Randin**, the cockeyed optimist.

**Adam**, more deserving than he thinks.

And to **Bram**, who loves me—but…

# INTRODUCTION

I've been making costumes since I was twelve years old. I didn't always know exactly what I was doing, but I was fearless, enthusiastic, and a bit bossy—which often led to me being put in charge of costumes. When I started working in costume shops, I sometimes found myself running things simply because I was the only one who knew how to sew—a common reality in high schools, small universities, and community theatres.

At times, this was frustrating because:

1. My only formal sewing training came from middle-school Home Economics, so I often lacked the advanced skills I needed.

2. Theatre production schedules are unforgiving, leaving little time to teach an amateur costume crew how to sew before costumes are due.

When I began teaching costuming at the university level, I finally had the time to properly teach my students how to sew. However, both my students and I occasionally overestimated their skill levels—which sometimes led to, let's just say, unintended design choices. To address this, I created a series of "Skills Exercises" that students had to pass before they could work on actual costumes.

My next challenge was finding a beginner-friendly sewing book that broke skills down to their absolute basics—something designed for costumers with little or no prior experience. There are fantastic sewing resources out there, such as *The Costume Technician's Handbook* by Rosemary Ingham & Liz Covey and *Costume Construction* by Katherine Strand-Evans, both of which I highly recommend. However, I needed something even more foundational—a guide that someone without a mentor or teacher could use to learn the fundamentals in just a few weeks. So, I took my Skills Exercises, broke them down into their most essential steps, expanded them, and addressed the surprising questions I've encountered over the years.

This book is the result.

I hope it will be a valuable resource for:

- Those new to sewing
- Beginner costumers navigating educational and community theatre on their own
- First-year theatre students
- Cosplayers bringing their designs to life
- Halloween enthusiasts crafting their perfect look
- LARPers creating immersive costumes
- And, of course, the teachers guiding them all

My goal is to help beginners let go of frustration and self-doubt and instead discover the joy and inspiration in sewing that I do. To all my students who have been my guinea pigs for this book—who have patiently practiced (and even taught) the Skills Exercises over the years—THANK YOU.

# SEWING COMMANDMENTS

5/8

### USE A 5/8" SEAM ALLOWANCE

A 5/8" seam allowance isn't just a good idea—it's the law. It can mean the difference between a perfectly fitted garment and a lopsided disaster.

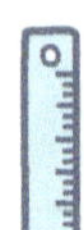

### USE STANDARD STITCH LENGTH

Standard stitch length = 10-12 stitches per inch (setting 3 on our machines).
Too small? Impossible to remove.
Too large? Falls apart too easily.
Stick to the standard.

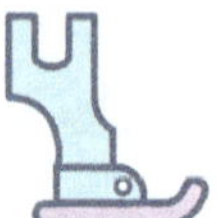

### LOWER THE PRESSER FOOT

Lower. Your. Presser. Foot.
If you forget, the fabric won't move, and you'll sit there wondering why.

### STOP IF THINGS GET WEIRD

Weird noises? STOP SEWING IMMEDIATELY and figure out why before you make things worse.

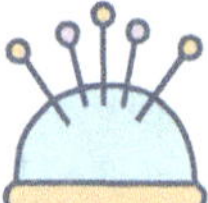

### USE PINS—THEY'RE YOUR FRIENDS

A skilled stitcher isn't someone who sews without pins. It's someone who uses them to keep things from shifting.

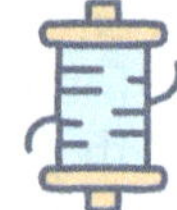

### PLAN AHEAD WITH THREAD

When hand-stitching, always check how much thread you have left. Leave enough for an anchor stitch and a knot—unless you enjoy unnecessary frustration.

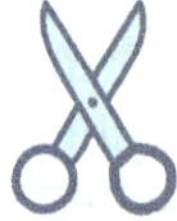

### TRIM THREAD TAILS

Loose thread tails look messy, get in the way, and scream, "I don't care about my work." Cut them off.

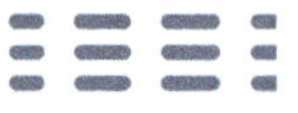

### NEVER LEAVE RAW EDGES

Always finish raw edges. They stretch, fray, and scream, "I wasn't taught properly." Hide your stitches whenever possible.

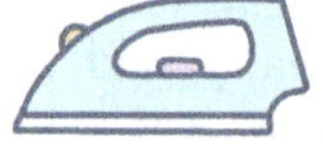

### IRON YOUR SEAMS

Press your seams. Always. I can spot unpressed seams from across the room, and yes, it makes that much of a difference.

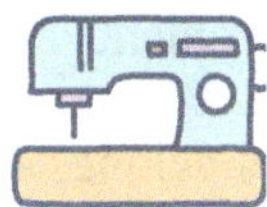

**RESPECT THE MACHINE**

Use the correct needles and bobbins. Otherwise, the machine will get upset. And an angry sewing machine is bad news.

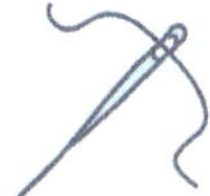

**THREAD PROPERLY**

90% of sewing machine problems come down to bad threading. 75% of my statistics are made up. Check your threading

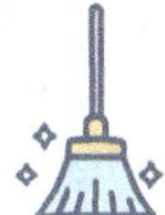

**DON'T BE A SLOB**

Clean up after yourself. A messy workspace slows everyone down, and I shouldn't have to stop my work just to clean up yours.

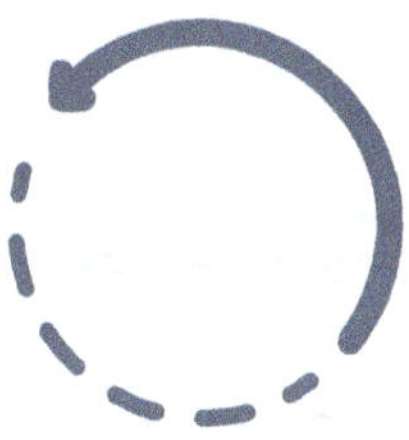

**BACKTACK AT THE BEGINNING AND END**

- Backtack at the start and end of seams you want to last—it's like tying a knot.
- DO NOT backtack excessively. It's overkill and a nightmare to rip out.

Backtacking is the process of sewing a few stitches forward, then reversing over them at the beginning and end of a seam to secure the stitches. It prevents the seam from unraveling over time. Think of it like tying a knot in thread when hand-sewing—it locks everything in place. If you don't backtack, the stitches can start to come undone with wear and washing. But if you overdo it, it can make the seam bulky and difficult to remove if you need to adjust something later.

## Safety Tips

- Keep your fingers at least one inch away from the sewing machine needle at all times. Accidents happen fast.
- Pay attention. Do not look away until the machine has completely stopped.
- Secure long hair, loose clothing, and jewelry to prevent them from getting caught in the machine.
- Listen to the machine. If it starts making a weird noise, stop sewing immediately and troubleshoot before continuing.
- Never put pins in your mouth. Seriously. Just don't. It's a choking hazard.
- Avoid sewing when tired, intoxicated, or medicated. Mistakes (and injuries) happen when you're not fully alert.
- Use the correct needle. A dull or incorrect needle can break mid-stitch, sending sharp metal flying. Change needles regularly.
- Unplug the machine when changing the needle, cleaning, or stepping away. Safety first.
- Keep scissors and sharp tools in a designated spot. No one enjoys an accidental hand stab.
- Make sure your workspace is well-lit. Straining to see what you're doing increases the risk of mistakes and injuries.
- If you're frustrated, take a break. The machine will still be there when you return, and a clear head is safer.

## Sewing Terminology: What Do We Call Ourselves?

- I don't like the word "seamstress"—not everyone who sews is female.
- "Tailor" isn't always accurate either; tailoring is a specialized skill.
- "Sewer" exists, but I always read it as the place where sewage flows.
- "Sewist"? Sorry, I just can't.
- "Seamster" is a valid gender-neutral option.
- "Sempster" is an older, timeless term that I personally love.

## Golden Rule of Sewing

"Measure twice; cut once."

Because fabric is a lot less forgiving than paper.

# NOTIONS

Notions are the essential items needed to complete a sewing project. Before we start, you need to know what each one looks like:

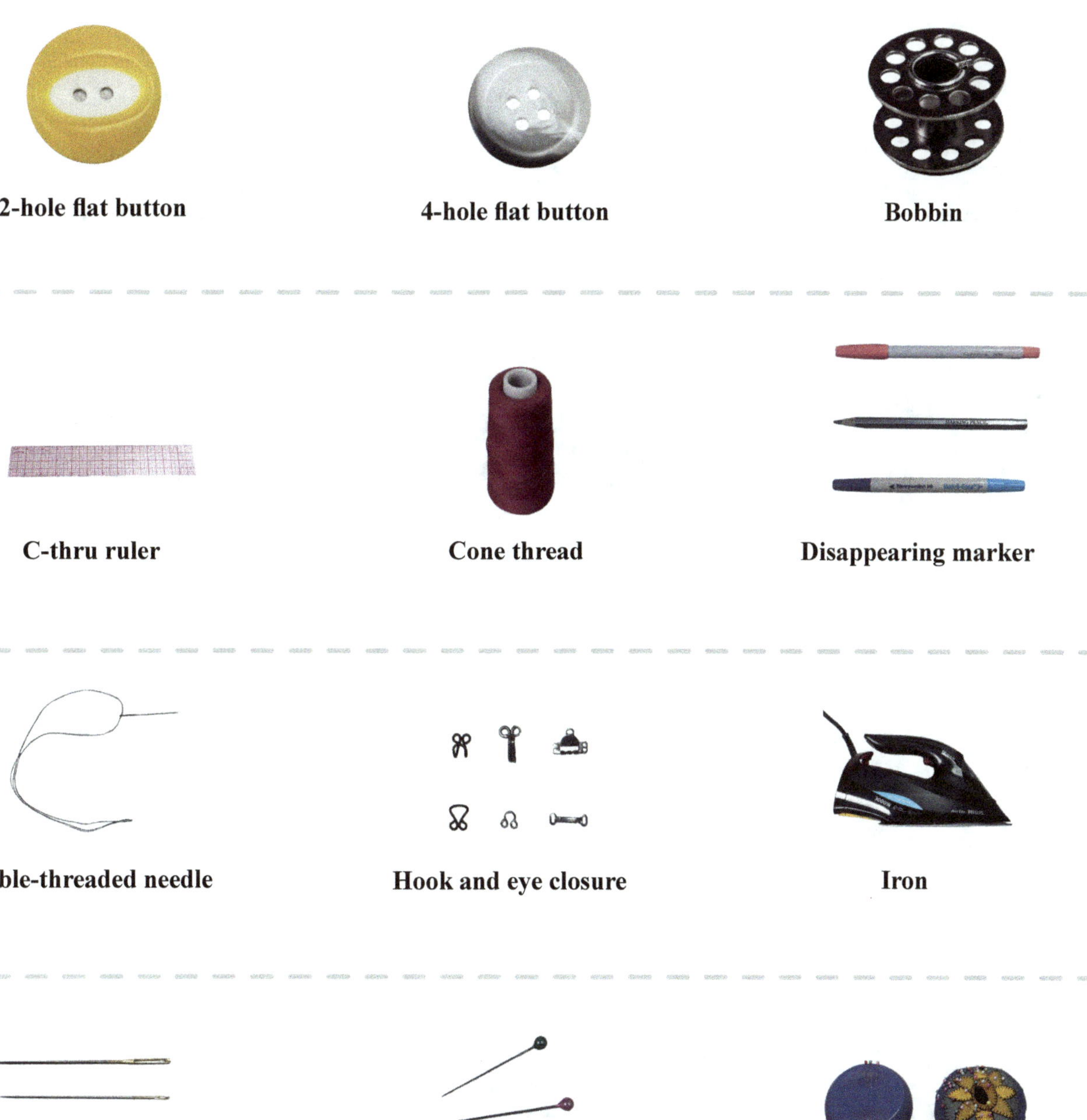

2-hole flat button

4-hole flat button

Bobbin

C-thru ruler

Cone thread

Disappearing marker

Double-threaded needle

Hook and eye closure

Iron

Needles

Pins

Pincushion

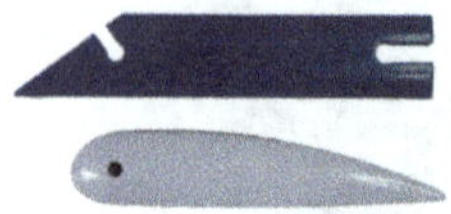

Point-turners

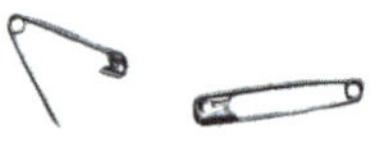
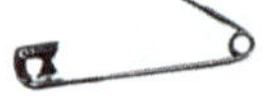

Safety pins

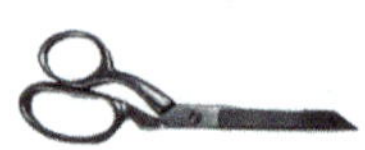

Scissors/shears

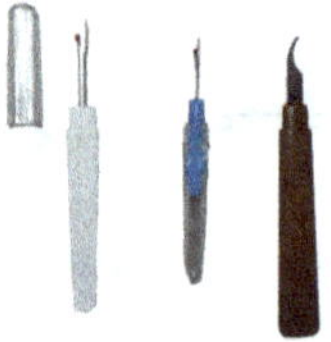

Seam rippers

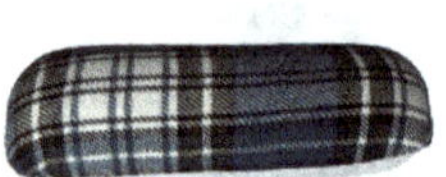

Seam roll

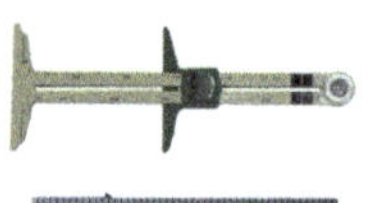

Sewing gauge

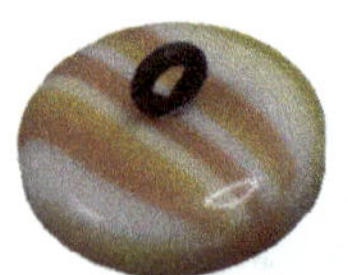
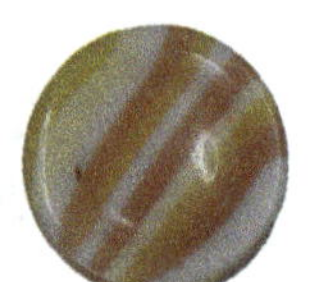

Shank button

Single-threaded neddle

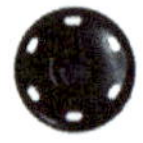
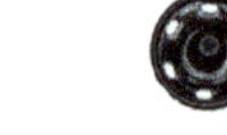
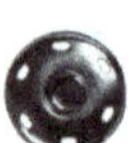
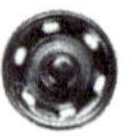

Snaps

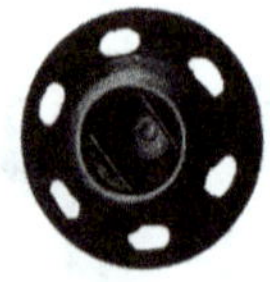

Negative snap (innie)

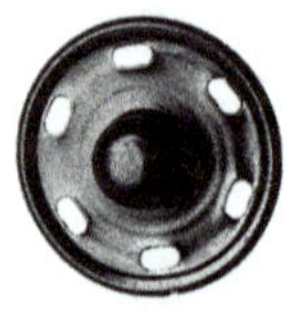

Positive snap (outie)

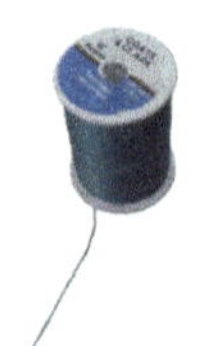

Spool thread

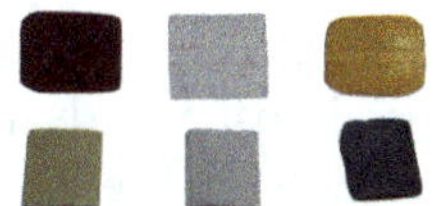

**Tailors chalk**

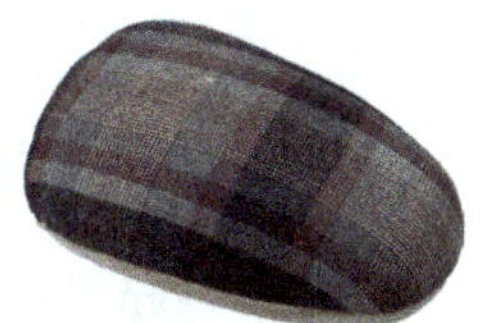

**Tailors ham**

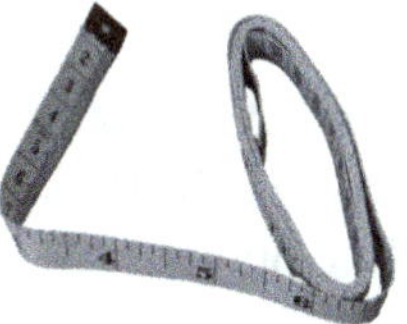

**Tape measure**

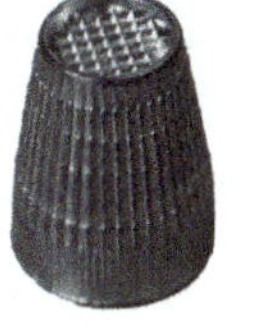

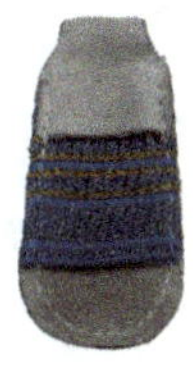

**Thimbles**

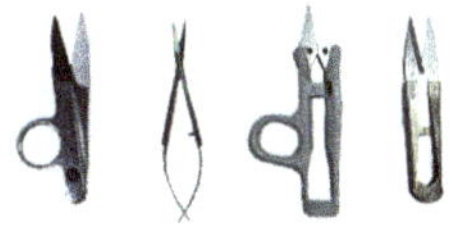

**Thread snips**

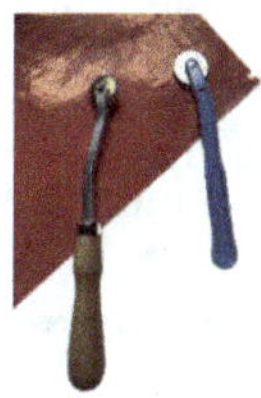

**Tracing paper & Tracing wheels**



11

# WHAT IS A SEAM ALLOWANCE?

The seam allowance is the width of fabric between the raw, cut edge and the stitched seam. Sewing fabric pieces together right on the edge isn't advisable—edges fray, unravel, and your garment will fall apart.

**Is There a Standard Seam Allowance?**
That's a *loaded* question. Seam allowances vary depending on:

- Who's sewing
- What's being sewn
- How the finished item will be used

Here are some common seam allowances:

- Quilters use a ¼" seam allowance to reduce bulk when multiple seams join at a single point.
- Muslin mockups often have a 1" seam allowance to allow for fitting adjustments.
- The fashion industry typically uses ½" seam allowances.
- Most commercial sewing patterns include a ⅝" seam allowance, making it the standard for home sewers.

**So Which Seam Allowance Should I Use?**
If you're drafting your own patterns, choose whatever seam allowance sparks joy. Just keep these rules in mind:

- Larger seam allowances allow for alterations but create bulk.
- Smaller seam allowances reduce bulk but leave less room for adjustments.
  Whatever you choose—stay consistent.

If you're using a commercial pattern, follow the specified seam allowance. If you're working in a costume shop, use the seam allowance set by the shop manager. Since I learned to sew at home (and most of my shop's team did too), my shops and all my patterns use a ⅝" seam allowance.

**Why ⅝"? That's Not a Very Round Number.**
There are many theories about why ⅝" became the standard, but my favorite is: ⅝" is almost exactly 1.5 cm. The rest of the world uses the metric system, so seam allowances are typically 1.5 cm—enough for alterations but not too bulky. In the stubborn U.S., ⅝" is the norm.

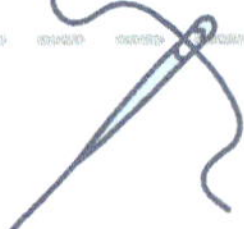

**Did You Know?**

- The wide end of a seam gauge measures ☒"
- Many tape measures are ☒" wide
- Most home sewing machines have a ☒" seam allowance line on the stitch plate

# SYMBOLS

Commercial patterns include symbols on the pattern pieces to prevent clutter from excessive writing and arrows. A symbol key should be provided on the instruction sheet that comes with the pattern.

Fortunately, most pattern companies standardized their symbols long ago, so you don't have to learn a new code for every pattern. Sempsters who create their own patterns also use these symbols.

Pattern symbols are like a secret code—understood only by those who sew.

## Pattern Symbols

- Notches
- Alteration Lines
- Straight Grain Line
- Cutting Lines
- Place/Cut on Fold
- Buttonhole Placement
- Button Placement
- Construction Detail Marks
- Right Side of Fabric
- Wrong Side of Fabric

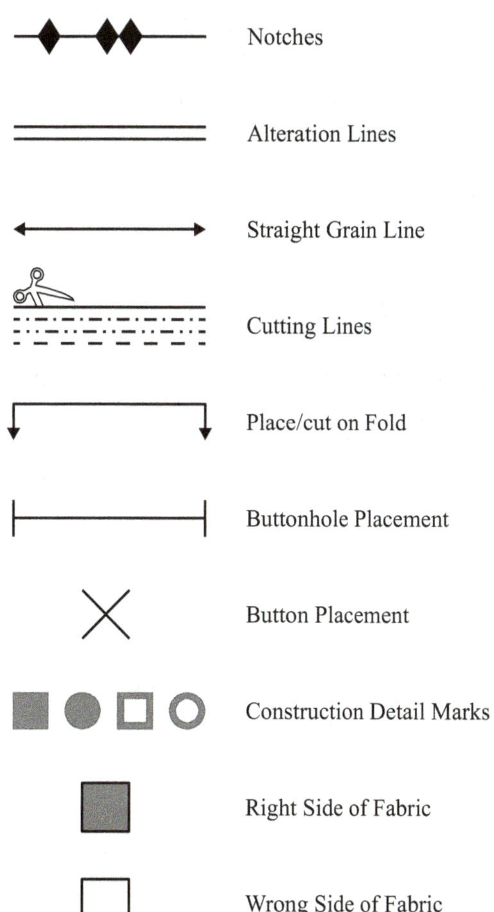

# FABRIC

Fabric, also called "material" or, more technically, "textile," is classified based on how it's made—its fabrication, if you will.

Woven fabric is created by weaving a set of longer threads running along the length of the fabric, called the warp, with a set of crossing threads running along the width, called the weft. Woven fabric has no natural stretch, except along the bias, unless it's woven with elastic fibers—like leggings and skinny jeans.

**Examples:** Calico, denim, flannel, suiting, corduroy, muslin, gauze, velvet, shirting.

Knit fabric is formed by interlocking loops of fiber, either by machine or hand. Knit fabric has stretch along at least one grain, while dancewear stretches in all directions.

**Examples**: T-knits, dancewear, sweaters, mesh, tricot, ribbing, velour.

Bonded fabric is made using heat, pressure, moisture, and/or adhesives to interlock fibers. This process involves pressing a mat of fibers together and working them until they become tangled. A liquid, such as soapy water, is usually added to lubricate and bond the fibers. Bonded fabric generally has little to no stretch.

**Examples**: Felt, polar fleece, interfacing, insulation, tarp, batting, padding, disposable clothing, hygiene products, diapers.

Knotted fabric is created by knotting, twisting, and/or braiding fibers together at intersections—interlacing and interlooping to form an open mesh.

**Examples**: Lace, net, macramé, trims.

There is so much more to learn about textiles—it could fill several books and courses. Some people dedicate their entire careers to textile creation. If you're interested, I encourage you to research further.

Fabric should be prepared before sewing. Ideally, it should be pre-washed in the same manner it will be washed as a finished garment. If it's a woven fabric, you may need to true the grain again. The fabric should be wrinkle-free and folded in half lengthwise. You can true your fabric by:

1. Cutting one end on the crosswise grain and hanging the fabric from that edge overnight.

2. Stretching the fabric on the bias until the grain is properly aligned.

## What Does "True the Grain" Mean?

The grain of fabric refers to the horizontal and vertical threads woven together to create the material:

- Horizontal threads = Weft (Cross grain)
- Vertical threads = Warp (Straight grain)

The warp and weft should form straight, perpendicular lines.

However, fabric can sometimes stretch out of shape, causing the grain to shift at odd angles. The straight grain of fabric follows the warp thread running down the length of the fabric. Warp threads are rigid and naturally want to hang perfectly vertical. If a garment is cut off-grain, it will hang unevenly as the warp threads try to correct themselves. Weft threads (cross grain) aren't as stubborn as warp threads, but they still prefer to stay horizontal.

## Why Does Grain Alignment Matter?

Proper grain alignment is crucial for a garment to fit properly and maintain its shape.

Ever had a T-shirt or pair of jeans that twisted around your body when you wore them? That's because the garment was cut off-grain. To prevent twisting, fabric must be trued before cutting.

A simple trick: Woven fabric will rip along the grain, making it easy to determine true grain alignment.



15

# PARTS OF A SEWING MACHINE

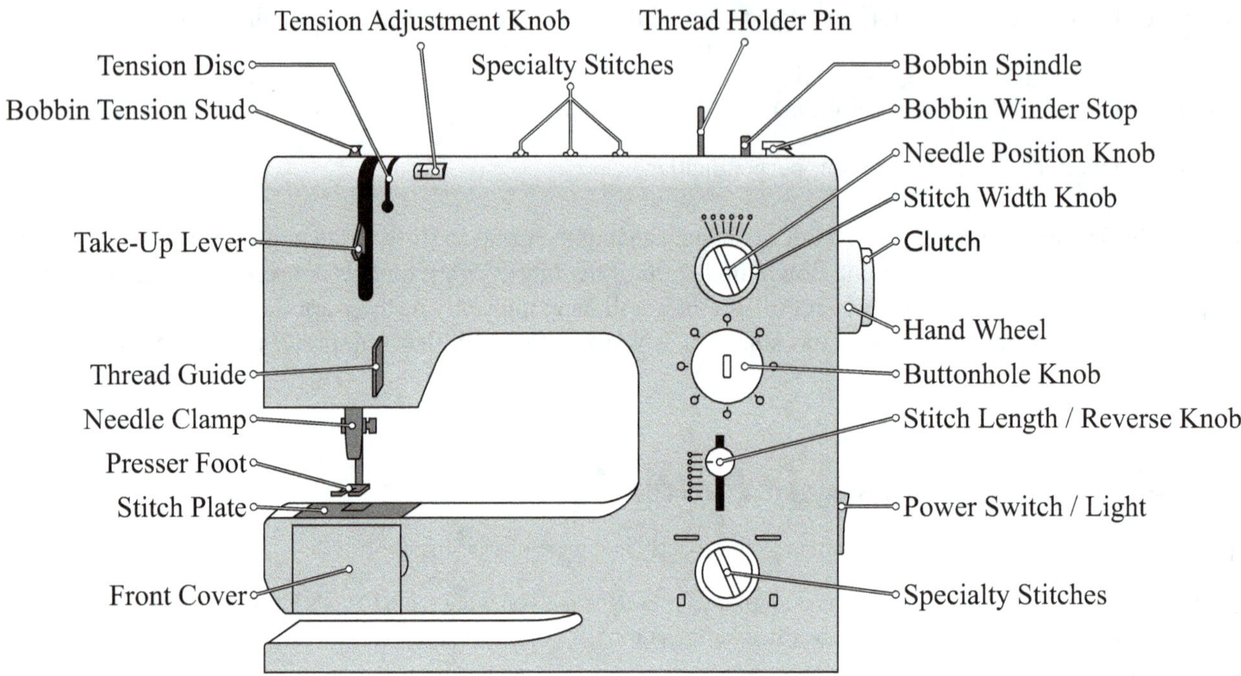


- Tension Disc
- Tension Adjustment Knob
- Thread Holder Pin
- Bobbin Spindle
- Bobbin Winder Stop
- Stitch Width Knob
- Needle Position Knob
- Clutch
- Hand Wheel
- Buttonhole Knob
- Stitch Length/Reverse Knob
- Power/Light Switch
- Specialty Stitches
- Bobbin Tension Stud
- Take-Up Lever
- Thread Guide
- Needle Clamp
- Presser Foot
- Stitch Plate
- Front Cover

**Oh no! This is a picture of a Bernina 1008! I don't have that machine!**

**It's okay—the basic idea is still the same. The thread has to pass through the tension controls, the take-up lever, and the needle. It's always a 'down-up-down' pattern.**

RTFM—or, if you don't have one, just google your machine. (*Once, in the long-ago days before the internet, I guided someone through threading their machine over the phone with my eyes closed. That's how basic it is.*)

## BERNINA 1008 TOP VIEW

- Presser Foot Lever
- Bobbin Tension Stud
- Thread Guide
- Thread Holder Pins
- Thread Take-Up Lever
- Thread Tension Disc
- Thread Tension Adjustment Knob
- Specialty Stitches
- Bobbin Spindle
- Bobbin Winder Stop

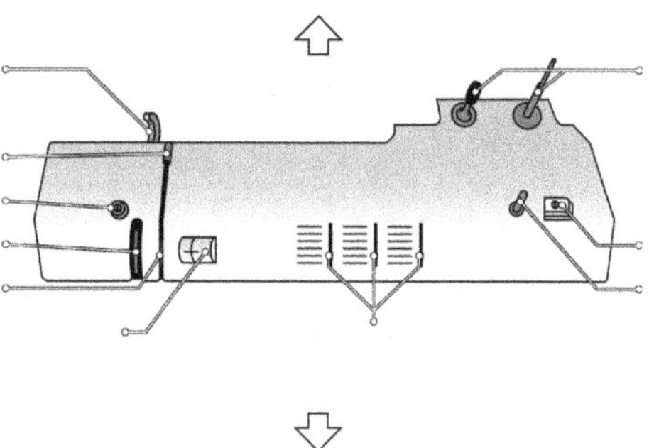

There are a whole bunch of specialty stitches available on a Bernina 1008. This is true for many other machines as well. These stitches are usually decorative and not used in everyday sewing.

Every time I want to use a specialty stitch, I have to dig out the user's manual because I don't use them often enough to remember how to do them.

If you're interested in fancy stitches for your sewing machine, check out *Sewing Machine Magic* by Stephanie Lincecum.

## BERNINA 1008 SIDE VIEW

- Bobbin Winder Stop
- Thread Holder Pin
- Hand Wheel
- Clutch
- ON/LIGHT
- Power/Light Switch
    - » ON
    - » OFF
- Stitch Width Knob
- Needle Position Knob
- Buttonhole Knob
- Stitch Length/Reverse Knob
- Specialty Stitches Knobs
- Power Cord/Pedal Cord Socket

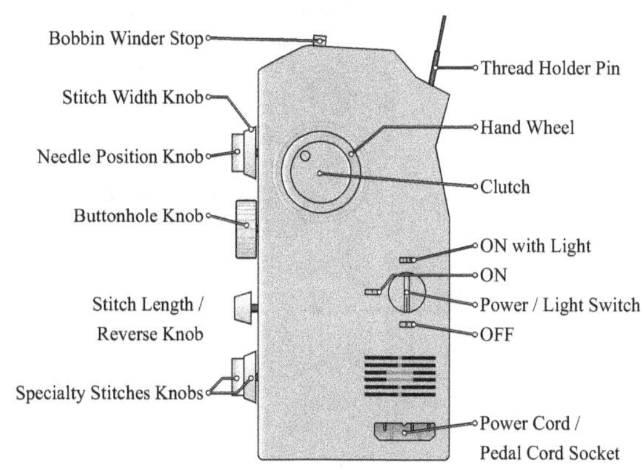

# MACHINE SEWING

**Why practice? Any fool can sew a straight line!**

Not true—I can't sew a straight line without a guide. And making a curve on purpose can be just as difficult. If you sew, you're going to be navigating a lot of curves and corners.

Use the spiral and square patterns provided to practice stitching on the machine without thread or fabric. Go slowly and get used to how the paper moves and the speed of the needle. Keep fingers clear of the needle space.

To make curves, use your fingers to gently guide the paper in the direction you want to go.

To turn corners on the square pattern:

1. When you reach the corner, stop.
2. Use the hand wheel to roll the needle into the paper.
3. Raise the presser foot and pivot the paper around the needle until the lines on the paper align with your next stitching direction.
4. Lower the presser foot and continue.
5. Repeat for each corner.

Repeat these exercises as many times as needed until you feel comfortable. Photocopy the pattern so you can practice as many times as necessary.

To remove fabric from the machine:

1. Use the hand wheel to lift the needle out of the fabric.
2. Grip the hand wheel as if you're about to shake hands.
3. Turn the wheel by twisting your wrist downward so your thumb moves down and under—NOT up and over.
   » This is the natural motion of the machine and keeps all tensions correct.
4. Cut the thread near the fabric.

**Need help? Here's a tip**: Lift your presser foot!

**Bigger tip?** Lower it again!

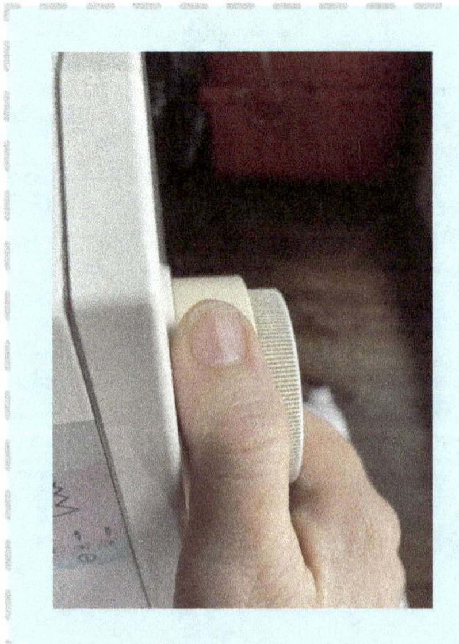

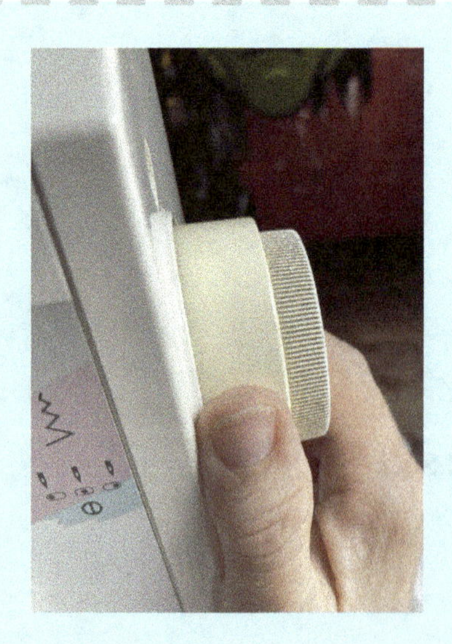

# EXERCISE

## SPIRAL PRACTICE SHEET

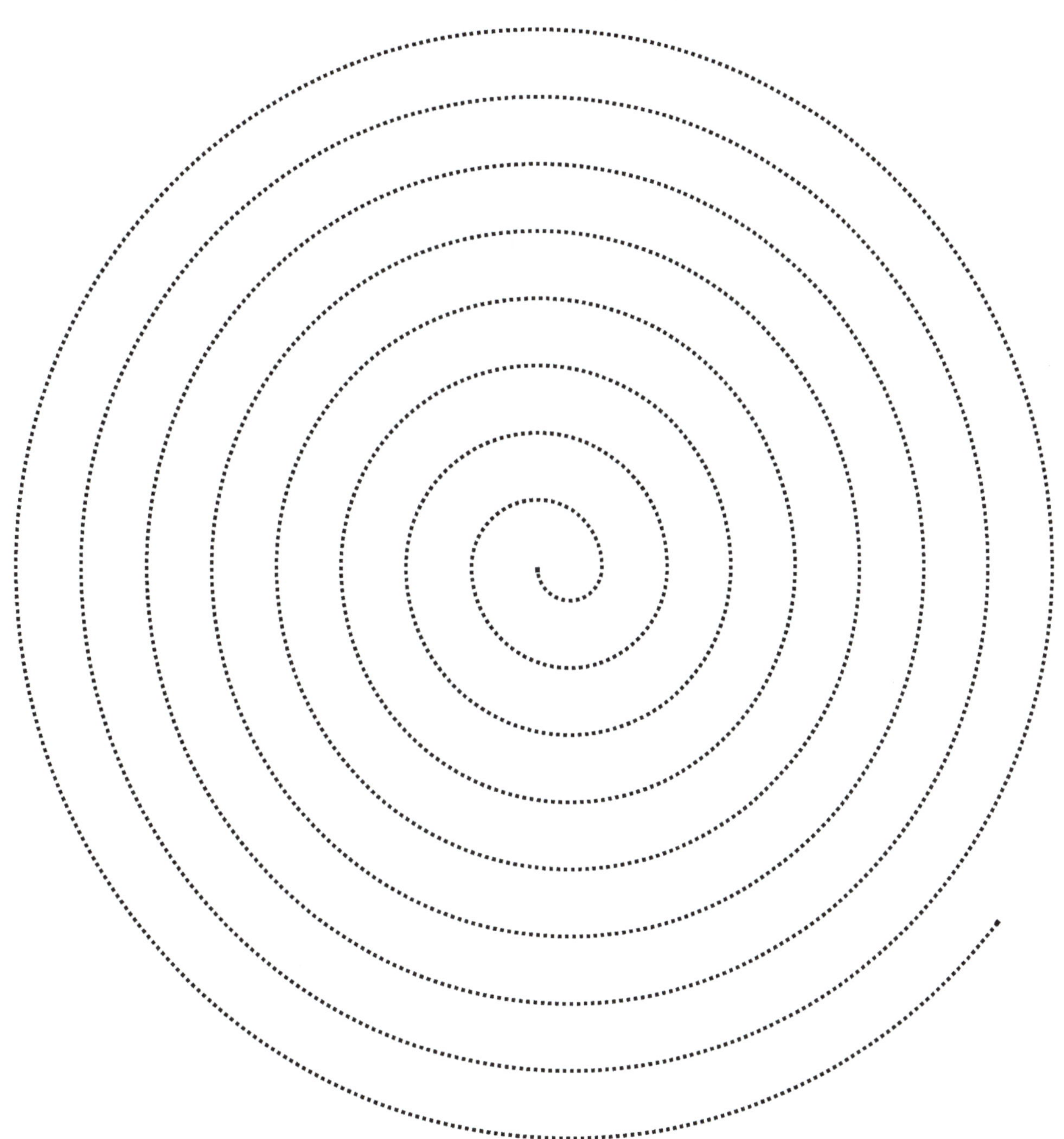

# CORNERS PRACTICE SHEET

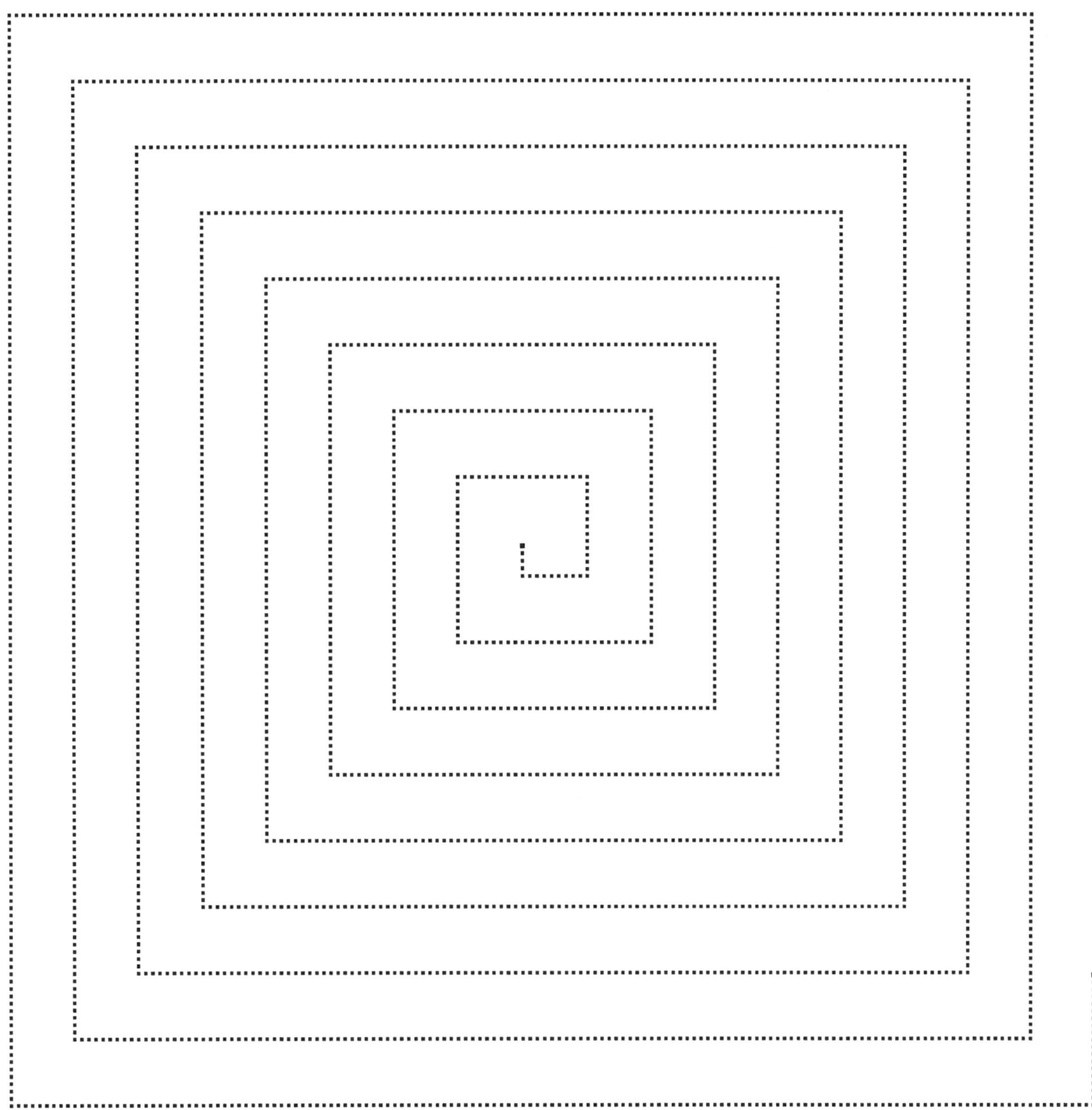

# THREAD THE SEWING MACHINE

Most machines follow a down-up-down threading pattern, known as the thread path. All machines share the same essential components along this path: spool pin, tension discs, thread guides, take-up lever, and needle.

Consult your machine's manual for specific threading instructions. If you don't have the manual, you can usually find threading guides online.

If your machine isn't sewing properly, the first thing to check is whether it's threaded correctly—because 90% of "my machine isn't working right" problems are caused by improper threading.

*(75% of my statistics are completely made up.* )

## Wind, Thread, and Take Up the Bobbin

The bobbin holds the bottom thread. Use the correct class of bobbin for your machine—this doesn't just mean plastic if your machine came with a plastic bobbin, but the exact class required.

To Wind the Bobbin:

1. Disengage the clutch.
   - » The clutch is the small wheel inside the handwheel (see *Side View Diagram*).
   - » To disengage: Hold the outer handwheel in place while turning the inner wheel counterclockwise until it loosens (about ⅛ of a turn).
   - » This prevents the needle from moving up and down.
2. Place your thread on the spool pin so it turns counterclockwise.
3. Wind the thread clockwise around the tension button—this keeps it from vibrating loose
4. Thread the bobbin:
   - » From the inside of the bobbin, place the thread through a hole in the rim and pull it out the top.
   - » Hold onto the thread lightly (don't grip it too tightly).
5. Place the bobbin on the bobbin spindle and engage the bobbin winder by pushing the spindle to the right.
6. Press the foot pedal to start winding the bobbin.
   - » Keep pressing until the bobbin is full—friction should cut off the loose thread you were holding.
   - » When full, the bobbin spindle will either pop back into position or simply stop winding.

Now Reverse the Process:

7. Pop the winder shank back to the left.
8. Cut the thread and remove the bobbin spool.
9. Tighten the clutch (NOT TOO TIGHT!)
10. If overtightened, it may tighten itself further while sewing, making it difficult to loosen later.
11. Thread your machine.

### Bobbin Winder Thread Path

1 Thread Spool

2 Bobbin Tension Stud

3 Bobbin

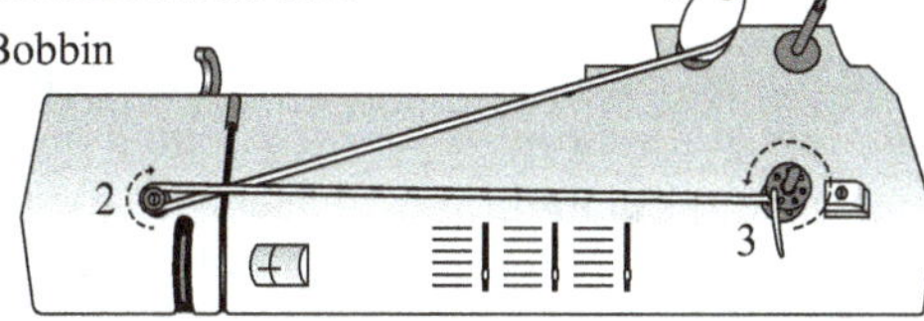

## LOAD THE BOBBIN

Place the bobbin in the bobbin case and insert the case into the bobbin cover.
The bobbin should spool clockwise.
Guide the thread through the tension nodes.

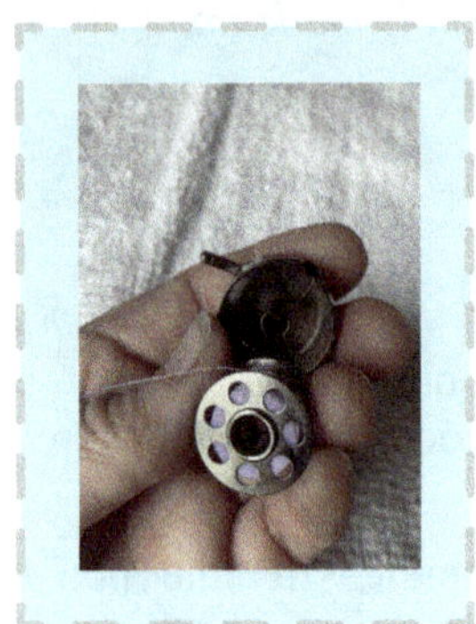

1. Place the wound bobbin in the bobbin case by aligning the bobbin spool hole with the bobbin case spindle.

» The bobbin should rotate counterclockwise when you pull the thread.

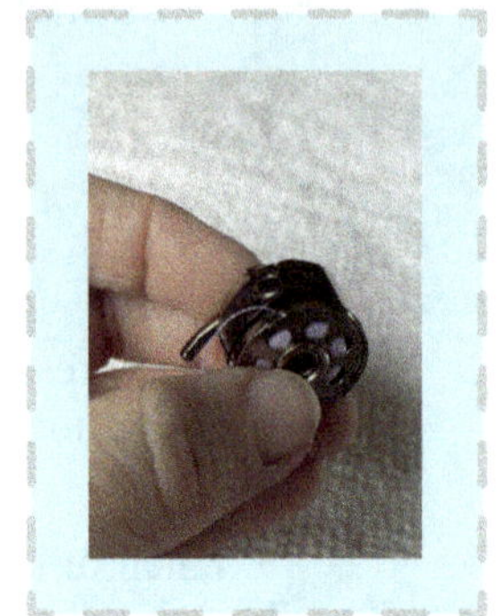

2. Put your thumb on the bobbin to keep it from moving.

» Pull the thread to the left until it reaches the slit in the bobbin case

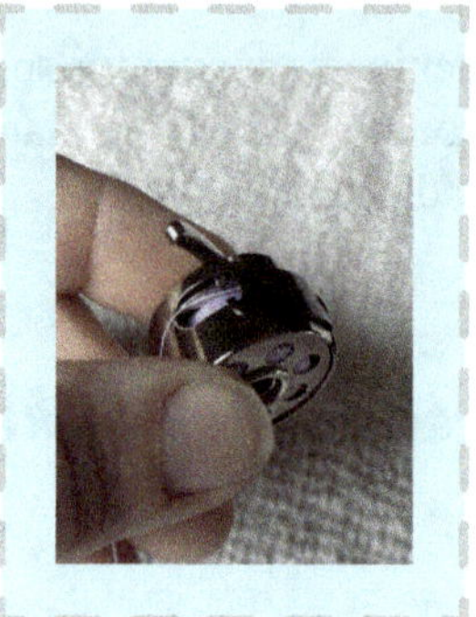

3. Pull the thread through the slit and continue pulling it left under the tension spring on the bobbin case.

4. Continue pulling the thread until it clears the tension spring and extends through the hole at the end of the spring.

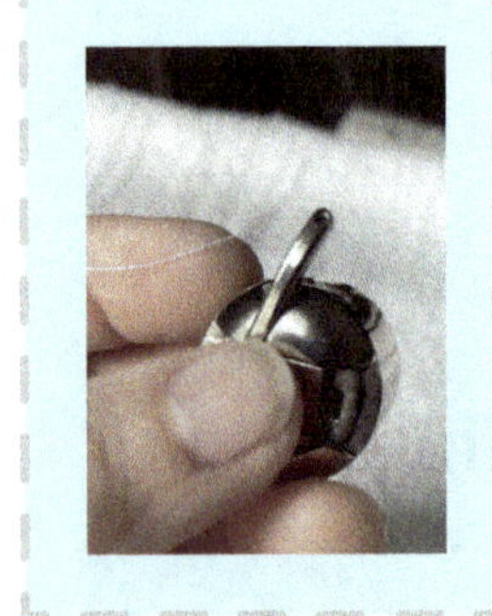

5. Lay the thread behind and to the left of the horn extending from the bobbin case.

6. Support the bobbin spool to keep it from falling out, then turn the bobbin case over so the top is facing you.

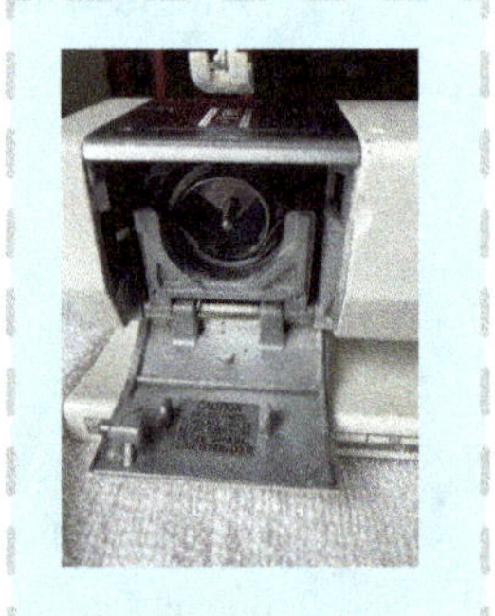

7. Place the hole of the bobbin onto the spindle inside the bobbin cover compartment.

8. Align the horn with the notch provided for it.

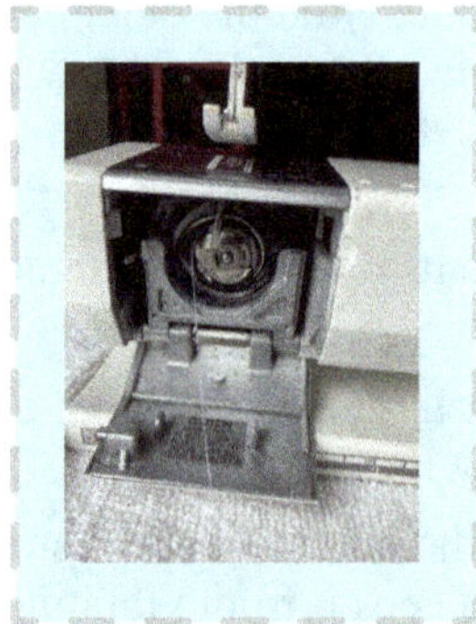

9. Push the bobbin case securely into place—you should hear or feel a small click when it's locked in properly.

## PULL UP THE BOBBIN THREAD

1. The bobbin thread needs to be brought up from the bottom of the machine to meet the top thread.
2. Hold onto the end of the top thread after threading it through the needle.
3. Turn the handwheel counterclockwise (*toward yourself*).
4. Continue turning the handwheel until the take-up lever has gone down and back up once.
5. Gently pull the top thread—both the top and bobbin thread should now be exposed.
6. Pull both threads under the presser foot and toward the back of the machine.
7. Leave about 6 inches of both threads past the needle.
   » If you cut the threads too short, the machine will unthread itself when you start sewing.
8. The threads should extend toward the back of the machine, away from you.
   » If they're left to the side or front, they may become tangled when you start sewing.

## FABRIC PREPARATION

For Samples:

- Cut 34 pieces of muslin, each 5" x 7", on the straight grain of the fabric.
- Use muslin that has been trued and ironed.

Why Use Muslin?

Muslin is the best fabric for learning to sew because:

1. It's inexpensive, so you can make mistakes without breaking the budget.
2. It's a woven fabric, meaning it won't stretch or bubble while you're learning.
3. It's sturdy, so it can withstand repeated seam ripping.

**Cutting Instructions:**

- Using a ruler and chalk, mark your fabric to cut 34 pieces of muslin (each 5" x 7") on the straight grain.

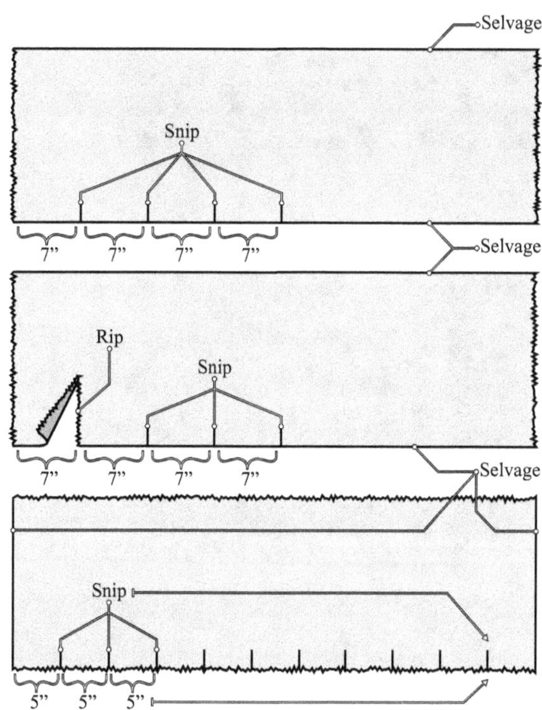

# MACHINE SEWING

Straight (Flat) Seams

- Sewn by machine with a stitch setting of 10-12 stitches per inch.
- Do not use smaller or larger stitches.
- Standard seam allowance: 5/8" (assume this unless otherwise indicated).

**Instructions:**

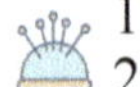

1. Use two pieces of fabric, each 5" x 7".
2. Place fabric right sides together, aligning the edges.
3. Pin along one long side, placing pins about 1" apart and at right angles to the edge.
4. Stitch a straight seam with the fabric edge at the 5/8" guide, backtacking at the start and finish.
5. Use the seam guideline to ensure even stitching.
6. Press the seam open.

This is the basic stitch used for most seam construction.

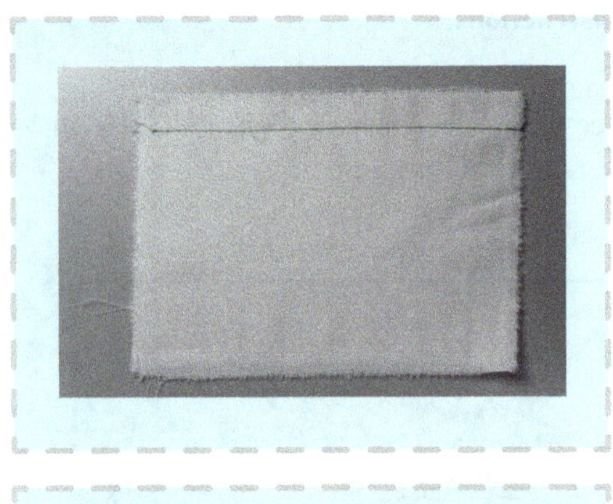

# CURVED SEAMS

## OUTER CURVE

- Sewn by machine with a stitch setting of 10-12 stitches per inch.
- Do not use smaller or larger stitches.
- Standard seam allowance: 5/8" (assume this unless otherwise indicated).

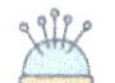 **Instructions:**

1. Use two pieces of fabric—cut into half-circle shapes using the pattern.
2. Place fabric right sides together, aligning the curved edges.
3. Pin along the curve, placing pins about 1" apart and at right angles to the edge.
4. Stitch along the curved edge at 5/8", backtacking at the start and finish, using seam guides to keep the stitching even.
5. Clip the curve.
6. Press the seam open.

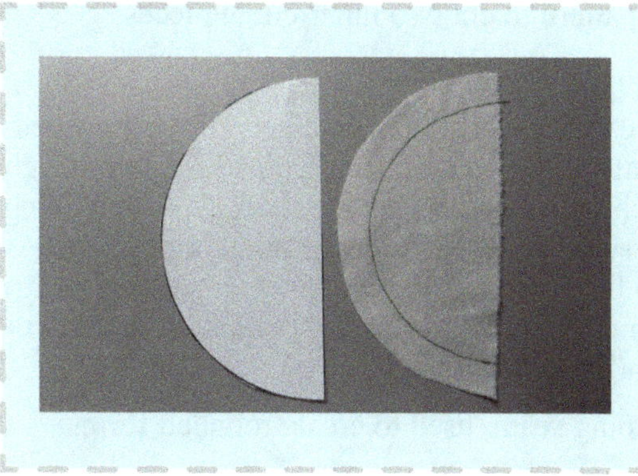

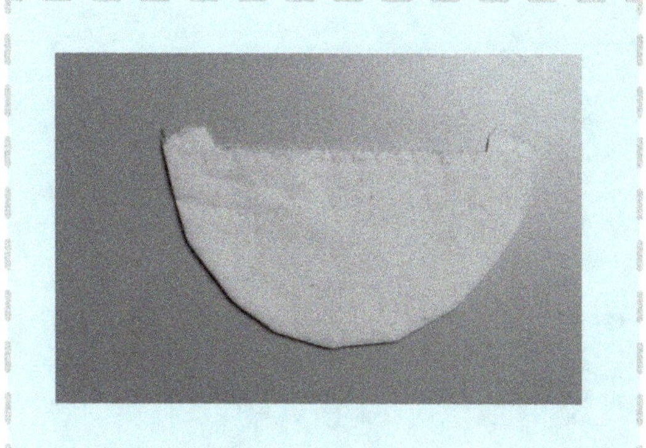

This is a shaping seam, used to create rounded forms in garments.

## WHAT DOES IT MEAN TO "CLIP THE CURVE"?

When you turn a curved seam right side out and try to press it, it may not lay flat. This happens because:

1. The inside edge won't stretch enough, or
2. The inside edge creates too much bulk.

To fix this, you must clip into the curve:

- Cut from the raw edge toward the stitched seam, creating small triangular notches in the seam allowance.
- Repeat this along the curve to allow the fabric to relax and lay flat.
- Cut close to the stitches—the closer you get, the easier the seam will press neatly.

# INNER CURVE

- Stitch setting: 10-12 stitches per inch.
- Standard seam allowance: 5/8" (unless otherwise indicated).
- Use two pieces of fabric.
- Use the pattern to cut two inner-circle pieces.

**Instructions:**

1. Place fabric right sides together, aligning curved edges.
2. Pin along the curve, placing pins ½" apart at right angles to the edge.
3. Stitch along the curved edge at 5/8", backtacking at the start and finish.
4. Use seam guides to keep the stitching even.
5. Clip the curve.
6. Turn right side out, so the wrong sides are together and the curve becomes an outer edge.
7. Press the seam.

This is a shaping seam, used to create rounded forms.

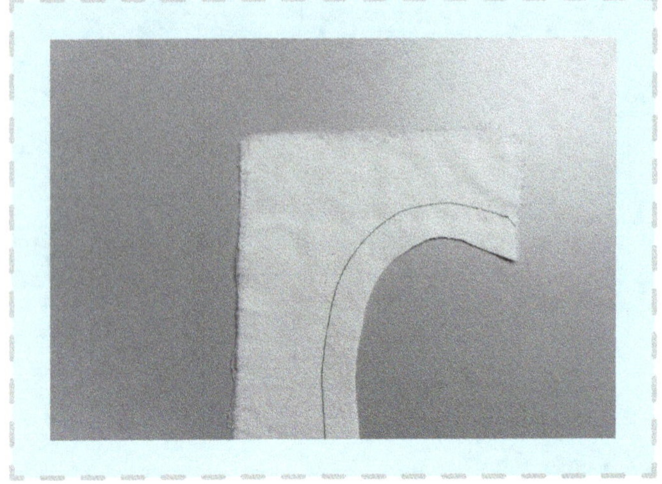

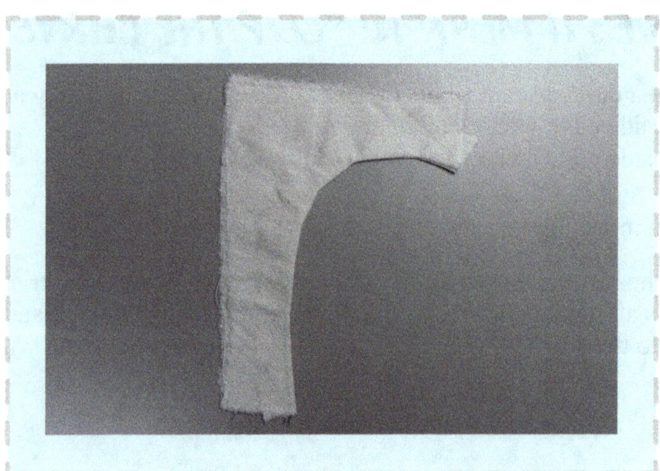

# CORNER SEAMS

## OUTER CORNER

Outside Corner

- Stitch setting: 10-12 stitches per inch.
- Standard seam allowance: 5/8" (unless otherwise indicated).
- Use two pieces of fabric.

 **Instructions:**

1. Place fabric right sides together, aligning one long and one short side.
2. Pin along the edges, placing pins 1" apart at right angles.
3. Stitch a straight 5/8" seam, backtacking at the start.
4. When you reach 5/8" from the end, stop.
   » Use the handwheel to roll the needle into the fabric.
5. Raise the presser foot and pivot the fabric around the needle until the short edge aligns with the 5/8" stitching guide.
6. Lower the presser foot and continue stitching, backtacking at the end.
7. Clip the corner.
8. Turn right side out and use a point turner to make the corner sharp.
9. Press the seam.

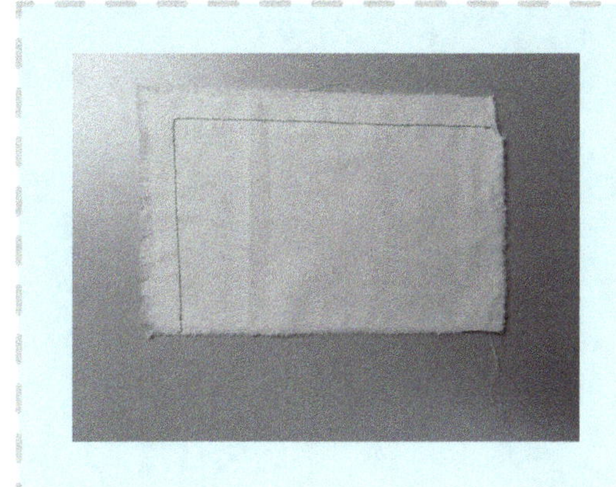

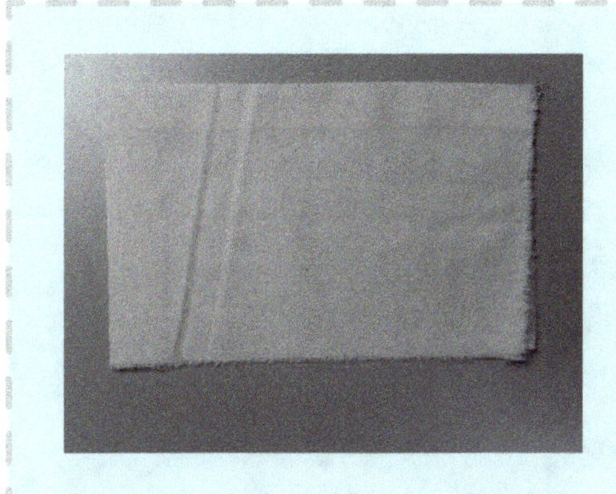

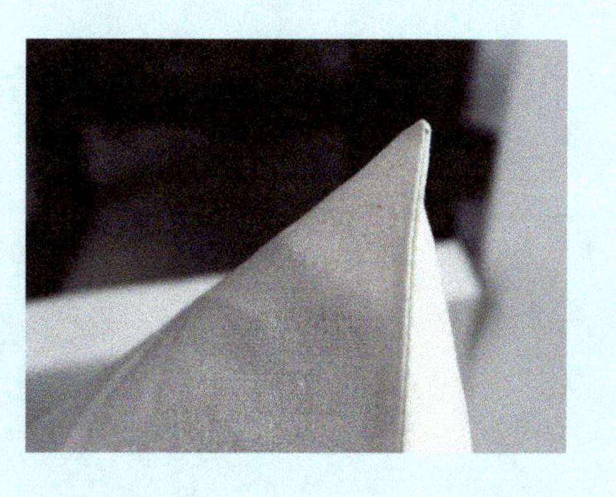

# INSIDE CORNER

- Stitch setting: 10-12 stitches per inch.
- Standard seam allowance: 5/8” (unless otherwise indicated).
- Use two pieces of fabric.

 **Instructions:**

1. Place fabric right sides together, aligning one long and one short side.
2. Pin along the edges, placing pins 1” apart at right angles.
3. Stitch a straight 1” seam, backtacking at the start.
4. To turn the corner:
   » Stop 1” from the end.
   » Use the handwheel to roll the needle into the fabric.
   » Raise the presser foot and pivot the fabric until the short edge aligns with the 1” stitching guide.
   » Lower the presser foot and continue stitching.
5. Stitch all the way around the fabric, creating a stitched rectangle.
6. Backtack at the end.
7. Clip inside the rectangle on the dotted lines.
8. Turn right side out.
9. Press the seam.

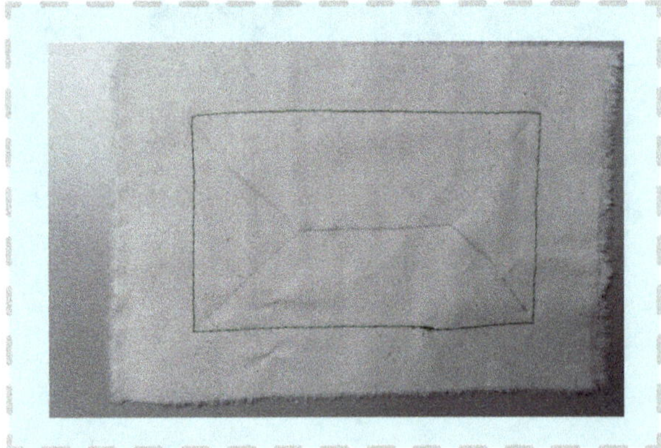

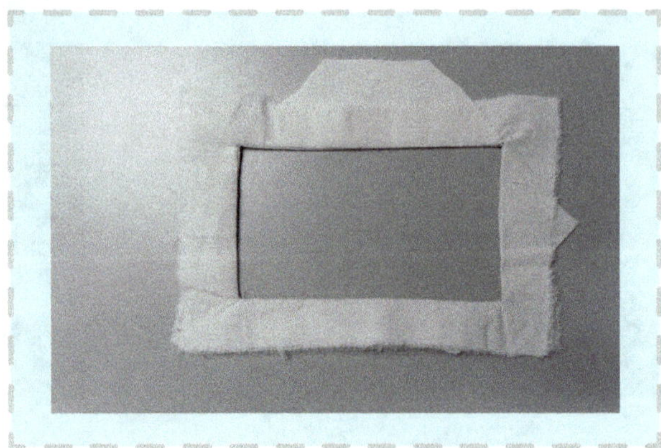

# TOP STITCH

- Sewn by machine.
- Use two pieces of fabric, right sides together.
- Standard seam allowance: 5/8".

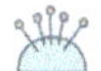 **Instructions:**

1. Pin the fabric layers together.
2. Sew a straight seam at 5/8", using a standard stitch length.
3. Press the seam open.
4. Fold along the seam, so the wrong sides are together.
5. Press the seam again.
6. Pin along the finished edge.
7. Sew along the finished edge at a 1/8" seam allowance, backtacking at both ends.

This is a finishing/decorative stitch.

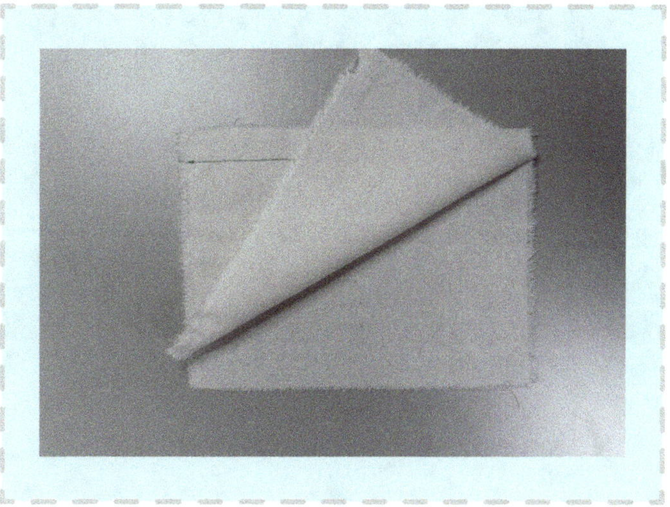

# DARTS

## STRAIGHT DART

- Sewn by machine.
- Use one piece of fabric and the pattern provided.

 **Instructions:**

1. Use tracing paper and a tracing wheel to mark the dart onto the fabric.
   » The traced lines will be stitching guidelines.
2. Fold the fabric along the center of the dart, with the traced lines on the outside.
3. Pin at right angles to the stitching lines, ensuring the lines match up.
4. Stitch along the seam line, backtacking at both ends.
5. Press the dart to one side (*toward the center of the garment*).

This is a shaping seam, used to create contours in garments.

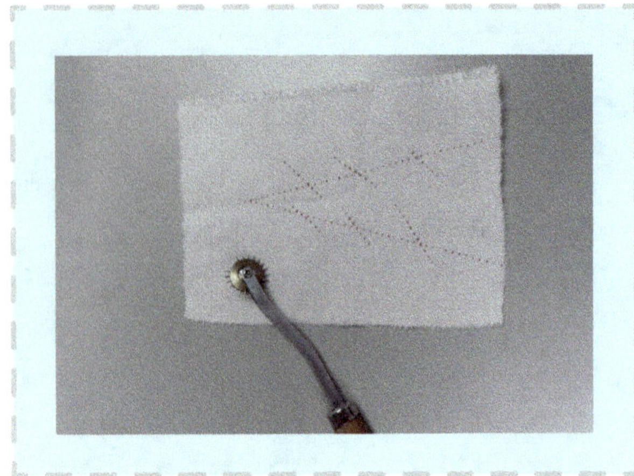

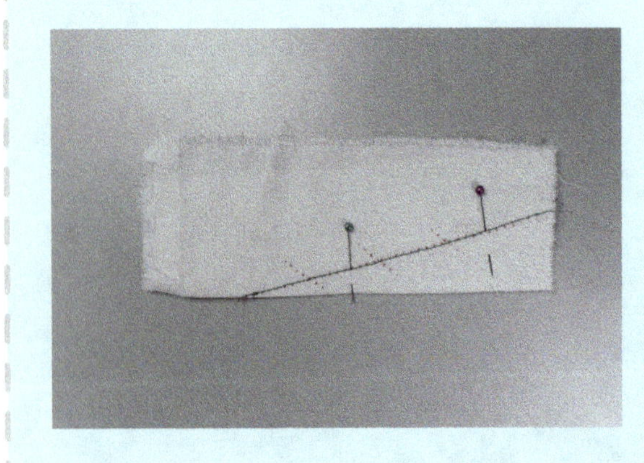

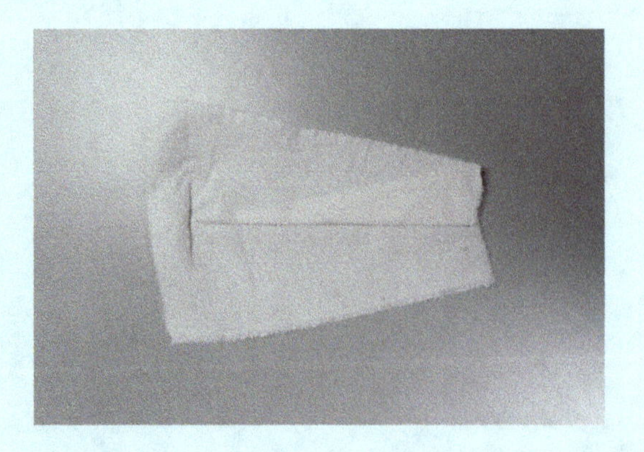

# 2-POINT DART

- Sewn by machine.
- Use one piece of fabric and the included pattern.

 **Instructions:**

1. Use tracing paper and a tracing wheel to transfer the dart pattern onto the fabric.
   » The traced lines will be stitching guidelines.
2. Fold the fabric along the center of the dart, with the traced lines on the outside.
3. Pin at right angles to the stitching lines, ensuring they align correctly.
4. Stitch along the seam line, backtacking at both ends and using a standard stitch length.
5. Press the dart to one side (toward the center of the garment) using a tailor's ham.
6. If necessary, clip the curve to help the dart lay flat.

This is a shaping seam, commonly used at the waist of jackets, dresses, and shirts.

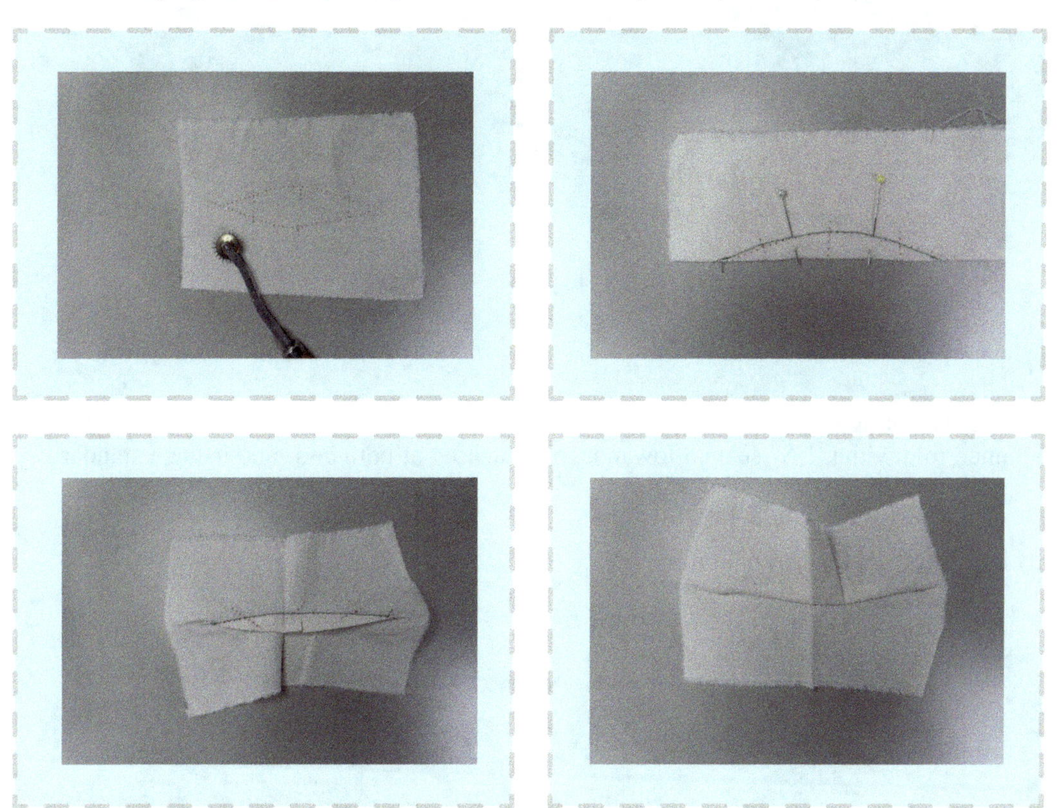

# FABRIC PREPARATION

For Machine Hem, Blind Hem, Catch Stitch, Machine Basting, Hand Basting, Buttons, Snaps, and Hook & Eye, prepare your fabric as follows:

1. Use one piece of fabric.
2. With the wrong side facing up, use a seam gauge and an iron to fold over one long edge by ¼".
3. Use the seam gauge and iron to fold the same edge over another inch. 01
4. Pin the free edge at right angles to the fold. 02

01

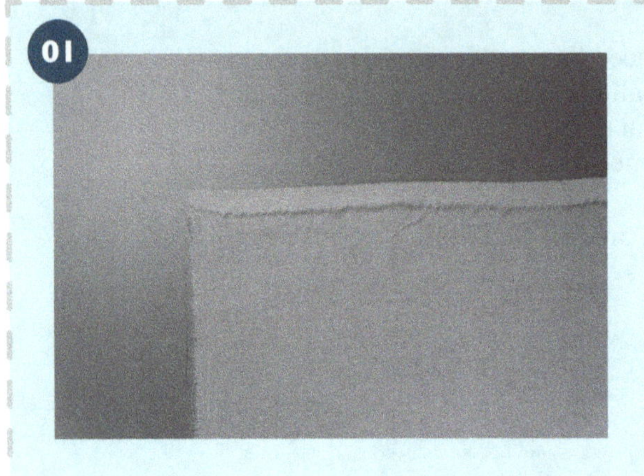

02

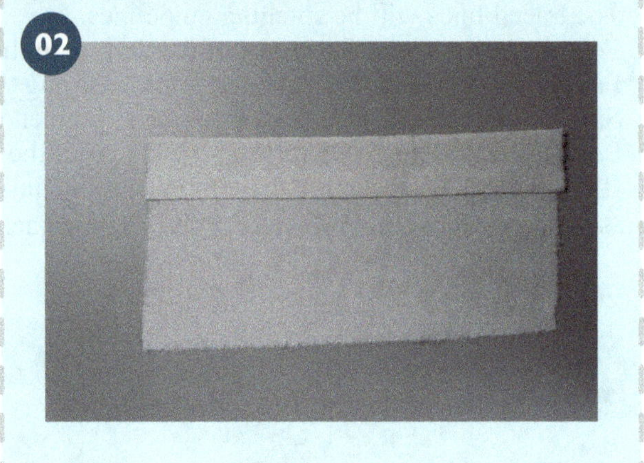

## MACHINE HEM

1. Prepare fabric as described above.
2. Stitch along the pinned fold with a 1/8" seam allowance, backtacking at both ends and using a standard stitch length.

This is a quick and sturdy but visible method of hemming.

Correct

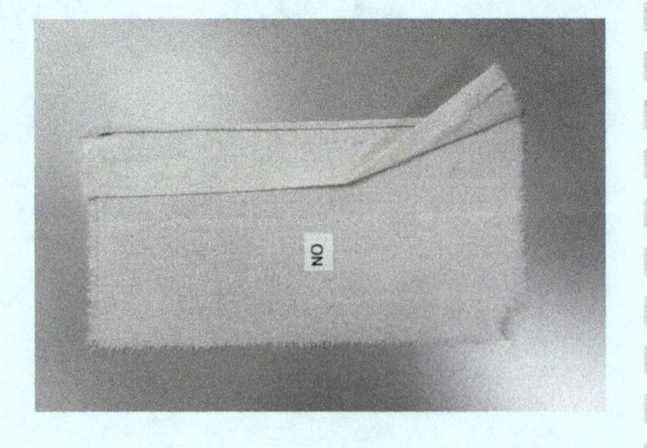


Incorrect

# MACHINE BASTING

- Sewn by machine using a basting stitch.
- Adjust stitch length to 5 (*the longest stitch setting*). This setting creates long, loose stitches that are easy to remove.

 **Instructions:**

1. Use two pieces of fabric, each 5" x 7".
2. Place fabric right sides together, matching edges.
3. Pin along one long side, placing pins 1" apart at right angles to the edge.
4. Stitch a straight seam at 5/8" seam allowance, but DO NOT backtack at the start or finish.
5. Use the seam guide to keep the stitching even.
6. Press the seam open.

Use a seam ripper to rip ½ of the seam open again.
Basting is used to temporarily hold fabric in place and is meant to be easily removed.

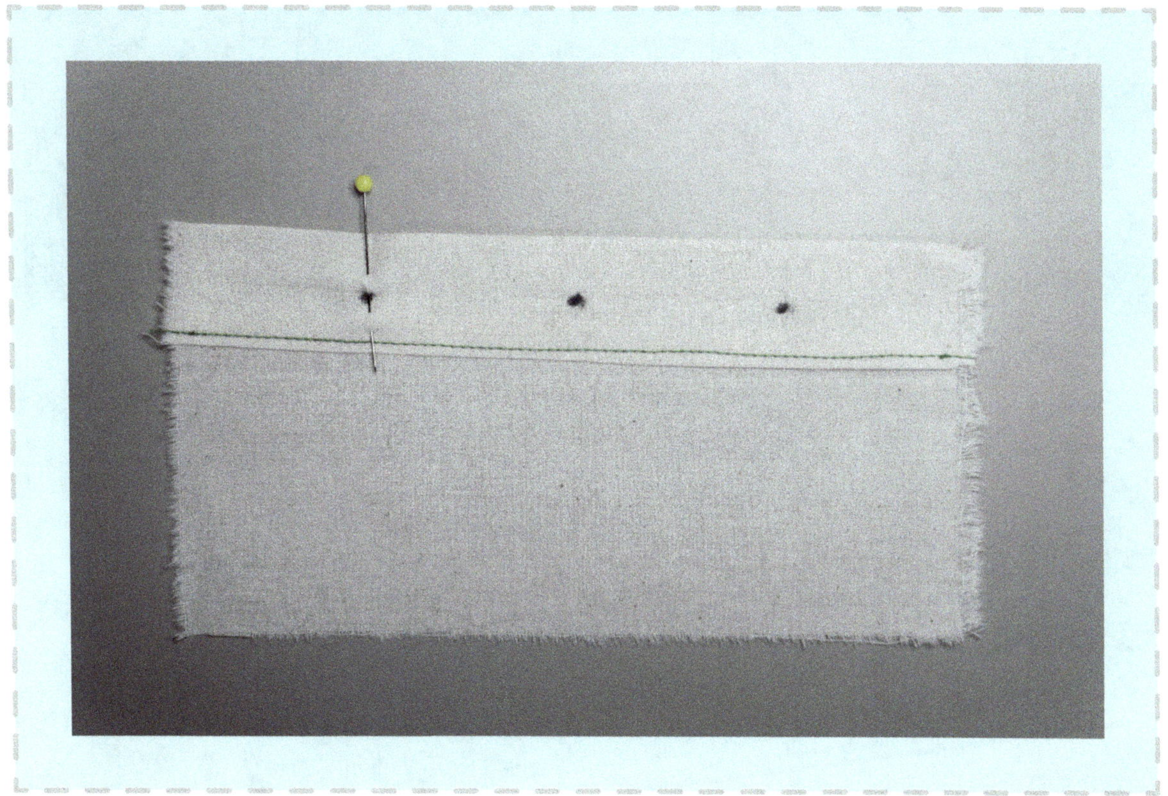

# GATHERING (SHIRRING)

- Use two pieces of fabric.
- Set your machine to its longest stitch length (5)—this is also called a basting stitch or gathering stitch.

 **Instructions:**

1. On ONE piece of fabric, stitch along the long (7") edge at 5/8". 01
   » Do NOT backtack at either end.
   » Leave a long thread tail on both ends.
2. Repeat the same stitch along the same edge, but this time at ½" seam allowance.
3. Pull up the bobbin threads to create an even gather. 02
4. Pin the gathered edge to the short edge of the second piece of fabric. 03
   » Ensure the gathers are evenly spaced and lay flat and vertical.
5. Sew at 5/8" seam allowance using a standard stitch length, backtacking at both ends.
6. Press the seam toward the gathers. 04
   » This stitch is used to create and control fullness in fabric. 05

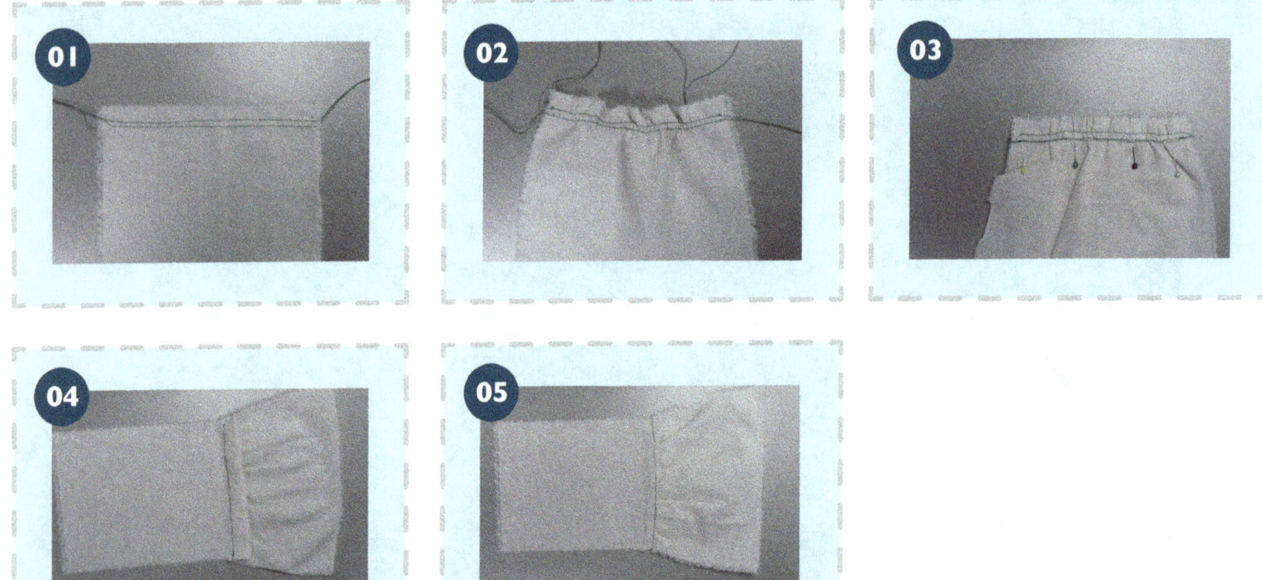

# BONUS: ADVANCED PRINCESS SEAM

**Princess Seam**
- Sewn by machine with a standard stitch length at 5/8".
- Use two pieces of fabric and the included pattern pieces.

 **Instructions:**

1. Match fabric along curved edges, right sides together.
2. Pin at right angles to the edge, using as many pins as needed.
   » It helps to pin the edges first, then the middle, then the middles from there, and so on.
   » Pick the pieces up off the table and visualize the shape three-dimensionally.
3. Align the seamlines at 5/8", not the raw edges.
   » If your seam allowance is 5/8" align the fabric at 5/8". Our smaple has a 1/4" seam allowance.
4. Stitch along the curved edge at the seam allowance. Backtacking at both ends.
   » Use seam guides to keep the seam allowance even.
   » Allow the fabric to curve naturally around the stitch plate arm.
   » Use your free hand to maneuver the fabric so it remains flat.
   » Go as slow as necessary.
5. Clip the curves and press the seam into the curve.
6. Turn right side out.

This is one of the most challenging seams in sewing. Don't worry if it takes a few tries! Princess seams are among the most difficult stitches and are also used to set in sleeves.

# PINNING THE PRINCESS SEAM

1. Pin one end, matching curved edges at ¼" seam allowance.
2. Pin the other end, matching curved edges at ¼" seam allowance.
3. Match the notches together and pin.
4. Pin the middle, matching the curved edges at ¼" seam allowance.
5. Continue pinning the middles, keeping the curved edges even with each other.
   » You will use a lot of pins.
   » The edges will look wobbly, but the curved seamline should be even and both fabric pieces should lay flat at ¼" from the edge.

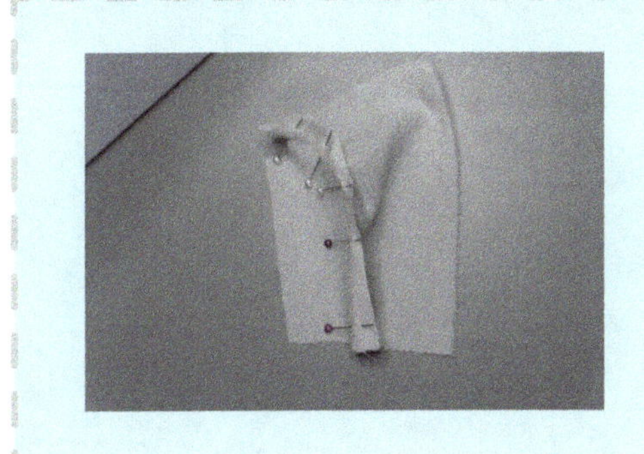

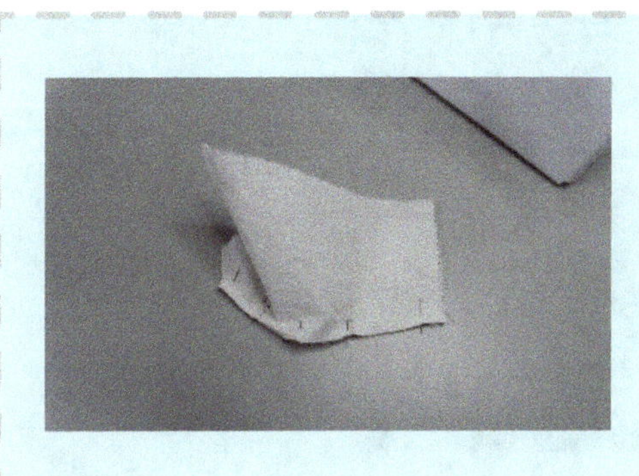

## SEWING & FINISHING

1. Stitch with a ¼" seam allowance. 01
2. Clip the curve. 02
3. Use a tailor's ham and press the seam toward the inside of the curve.
4. Turn right side out. 03

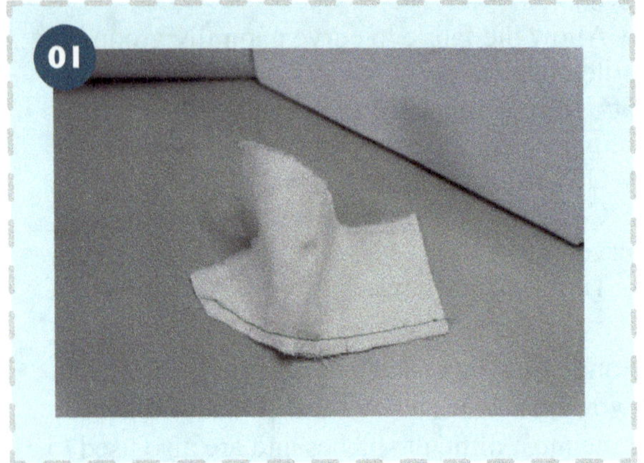

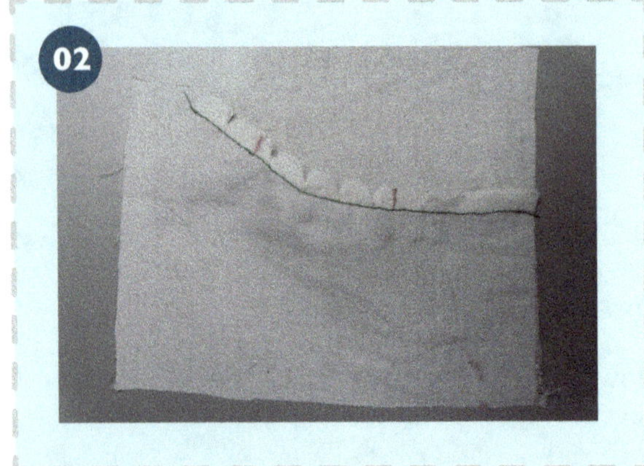

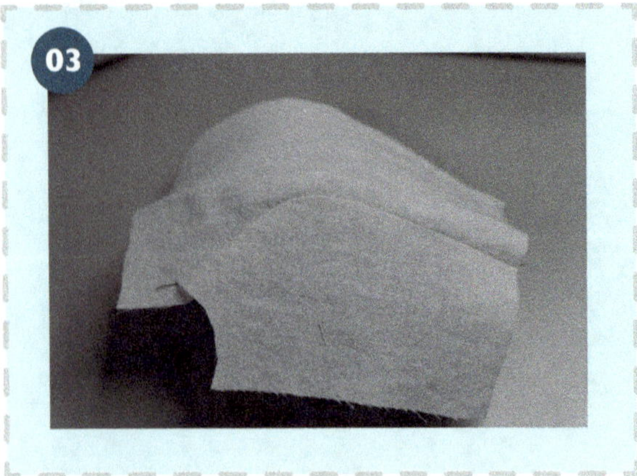

# HAND SEWING

Three Ways to Tie a Knot When Sewing by Hand

I have trust issues with knots, so I usually make a second knot in the same place. I also take anchor stitches (bring the threaded needle up through the fabric, move over slightly and take a small stitch back down), at the beginning and end. I really don't trust knots.

**Beginning to Stitch**

1. Thread your needle. Take the ends of the thread between your thumb and pointer finger, leaving about a 1" tail toward your palm.
2. Roll the thread around your pointer finger at least three times.
3. Use your thumb to gently roll the loop off the tip of your finger.
4. Pull the needle in the opposite direction, drawing the tail through the loop.
5. Voila!

**Alternative Method:**

1. Start with a threaded needle. Hold the thread near the eye of the needle so it forms a large loop.
2. Wind the thread around the needle three to five times.
   » The more you wind, the bigger the knot.
3. Pinch the wrapped thread near the needle.
4. Pull the needle away from you, keeping light pressure on the loops with your fingers.
5. Continue pulling until the knot forms.
6. Ta-da!

**To Finish Stitching:**

- Leave at least 3" of thread at the end to make a knot.
- Take an anchor stitch and bring the threaded needle to the top of your seam.
- Make a loop with the thread along the seam, following the stitching direction.
- Take another stitch, bringing the needle up inside the loop.
- Loop the thread around the needle 3-4 times.
- Push the loops down the needle and press your thumb on top of them.
- Pull the needle through, holding the loops in place.
- Voila! You have a knot!

# HAND BASTING (RUNNING STITCH)

The simplest hand-sewing stitch is the running stitch—you simply weave the needle in and out of the fabric at even intervals.

 **Instructions:**

1. Use one piece of fabric, a hand-sewing needle, and waxed Silamide thread.
2. Double-thread the needle.
3. Prepare the muslin as described in the Machine Hem section.
4. Make an anchor stitch:
   » Bring the threaded needle up through the fabric.
   » Move over slightly and take a small stitch back down.
   » Bring the needle back up near the first stitch—this creates an anchor.
5. Sew in a straight line along the 5/8" seam allowance, making ½" - 1" stitches.
   » I like to make my stitches slightly slanted so I can see them later when removing them, but that's optional.
6. At the end, make another anchor stitch, knot, and cut the thread.

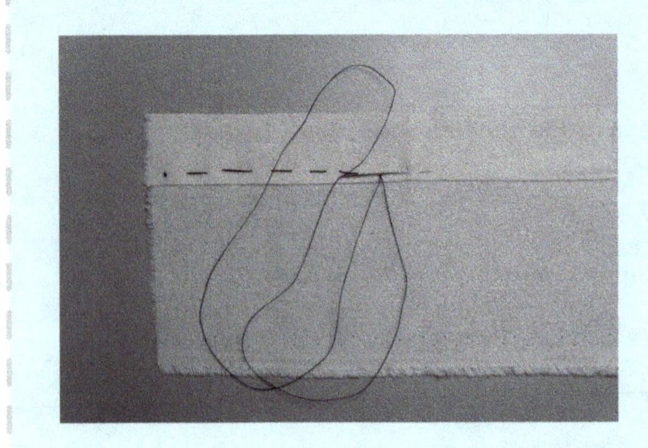

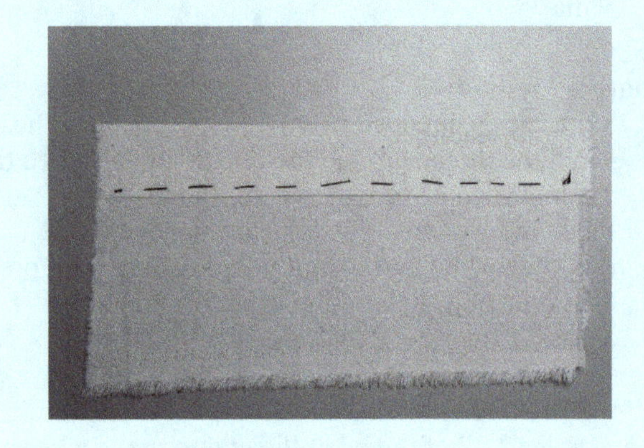

# BLIND HEM STITCH

This stitch is used for hemming woven fabrics.

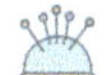 **Instructions:**

1. Use a hand-sewing needle and waxed Silamide thread (double-threaded).
2. Use one piece of fabric.
3. With the wrong side up, fold one long edge ¼" and press with an iron.
4. Fold over another 1" and press again.
5. Pin the free edge at right angles to the fold.
6. Make an anchor stitch.
7. Sew with a blind hem stitch:
   » Move the needle ¼" along the fold.
   » Take a tiny bite of fabric, catching only 1-2 threads.
   » Move the needle under the fold and travel through.
   » Repeat until you reach the end.
8. Make an anchor stitch, knot, and cut the thread.

This finishing stitch should be nearly invisible on the right side. If the thread matches the fabric, the stitches will be hard to see.

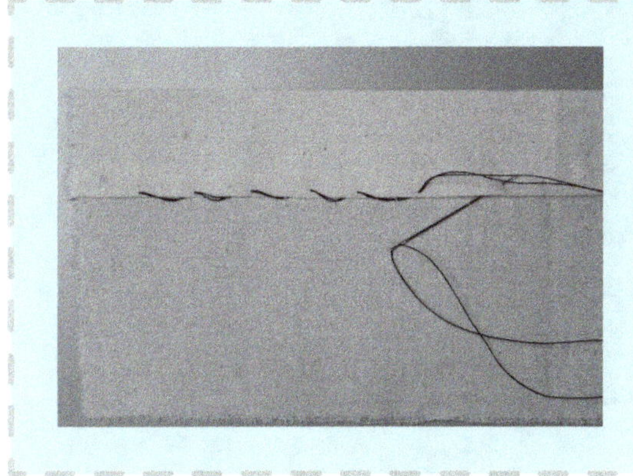

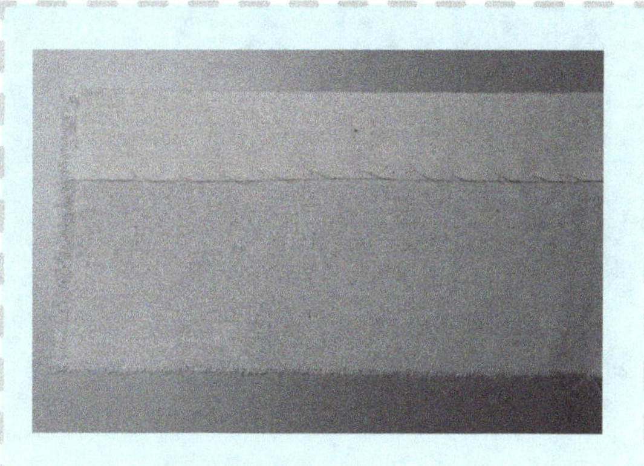

## Catch Stitch

This stitch is used for hemming knits, bias-cut garments, and securing facings.

 **Instructions:**

1. Use a hand-sewing needle and waxed Silamide thread (single-threaded).
2. Use one piece of fabric.
3. With the wrong side up, fold one long edge ¼" and press with an iron.
4. Fold over another 1" and press again.
5. Pin the free edge at right angles to the fold.
6. Make an anchor stitch.
7. Sew with a catch stitch:
   » Moving away from yourself (*but keeping the needle pointed toward you*), take a tiny stitch ¼" past the first stitch in the single fabric.
   » Move ¼" further and catch the fold from the top with another small stitch.
   » Continue moving away from yourself, keeping the needle pointed toward you.
   » The stitches should create a series of "X" shapes.
8. Make an anchor stitch, knot, and cut the thread.

This finishing stitch should be nearly invisible on the right side.

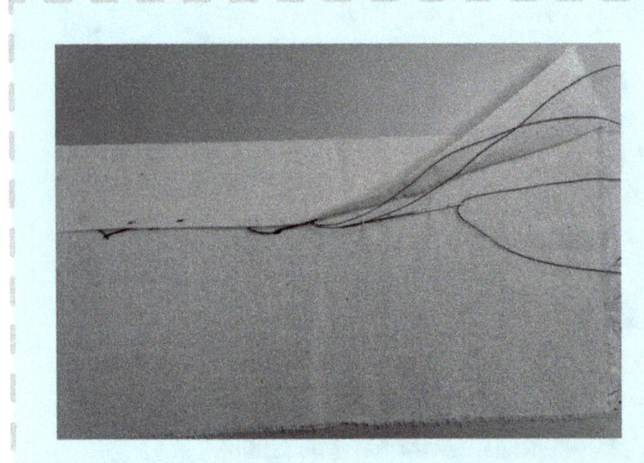

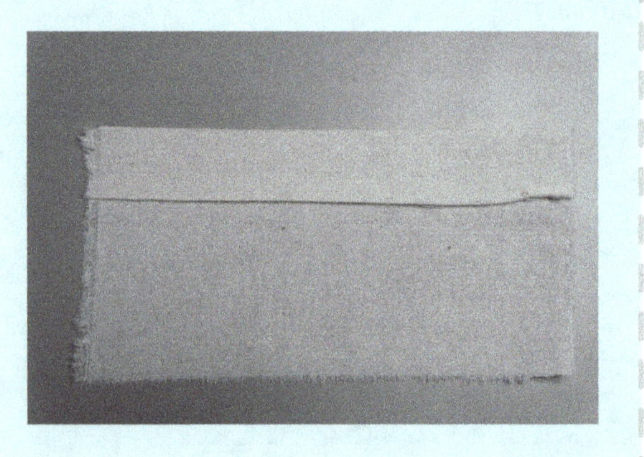

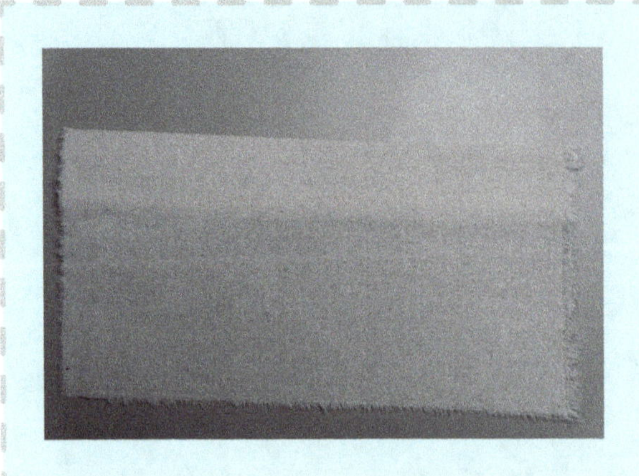

# BUTTONS

**Instructions:**

1. Use one piece of muslin.
2. Prepare a long (7”) edge as described in Fabric Prep.
3. Machine Hem the edge.
4. Mark the button placement:
   » Find the center of the band and mark it with tailor’s chalk.
   » Mark midpoints between the center mark and the edges.
   » You should have three marks equally spaced along the hemmed edge.
5. Use a hand-sewing needle and waxed Silamide thread (double-threaded).
6. Start with an anchor stitch on your mark.

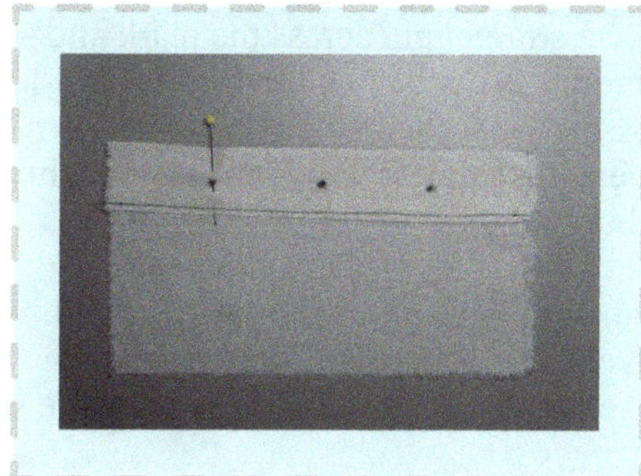

## 4-HOLE BUTTON

1. Place a straight pin across the mark and set the button on top of the pin.
2. Come up through the bottom of the fabric and through one hole with the needle and thread.
3. Cross to the second hole and stitch down through the fabric.
4. Come up through the third hole and stitch down through the fourth.
   » Your stitches should form either an “X” or an “=” shape on top of the button (*your choice*).
5. Repeat this process until you’ve gone through each hole 3-4 times, ending with the thread on top of the fabric but under the button.
6. Remove the pin.
7. Wrap the thread around the stitches 3-4 times to form a protective shield around them—this helps the button last longer.
8. Travel back down to the underside of the fabric.
9. Make an anchor stitch, knot, and cut the thread.

## 2-HOLE BUTTON

1. Place a straight pin across the mark and set the button on top of the pin.
2. Come up through the bottom of the fabric and through one hole with the needle and thread.
3. Cross to the second hole and stitch down through the fabric.
4. Repeat this process until you've gone through each hole 3-4 times, ending with the thread on top of the fabric but under the button.
5. Remove the pin.
6. Wrap the thread around the stitches 3-4 times to protect the stitching.
7. Travel back down to the underside of the fabric.
8. Make an anchor stitch, knot, and cut the thread.

## Shank Button

The process is the same as a 4-hole or 2-hole button, except you do not need a pin—the shank provides the necessary separation between the button and the fabric. The thread wrapping still serves to protect the stitching, making the button more durable.

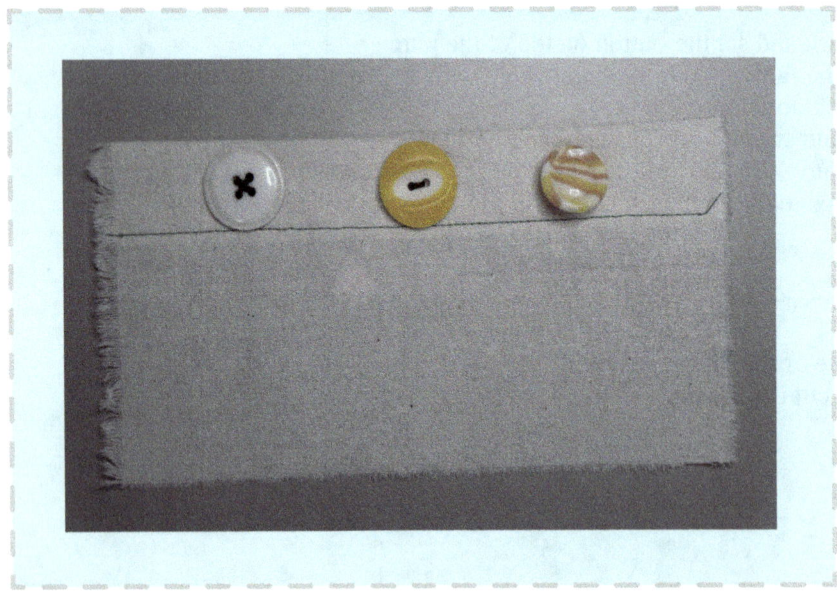

## Snaps

1. Use two pieces of fabric.
2. Prepare a long edge of each piece as you did for the buttons.
3. Mark the snap placement:
   » Use tailor's chalk to mark the center of the bands—on the outside of one fabric piece and the inside of the other.
4. Double-thread a hand-sewing needle.
5. Identify the snap halves:
   » Negative snap (innie) = The part with a hole/depression.
   » Positive snap (outie) = The part with a protruding nubbin.
6. Attach the positive snap:
   » Make an anchor stitch and sew the positive snap to the fabric.
   » Hide the stitches inside the hem where possible.
   » Sew through each hole 3-4 times.
   » Anchor and tie off.
7. Attach the negative snap:
   » Repeat the process for the negative snap on the other fabric piece.
8. Snap together to test alignment.

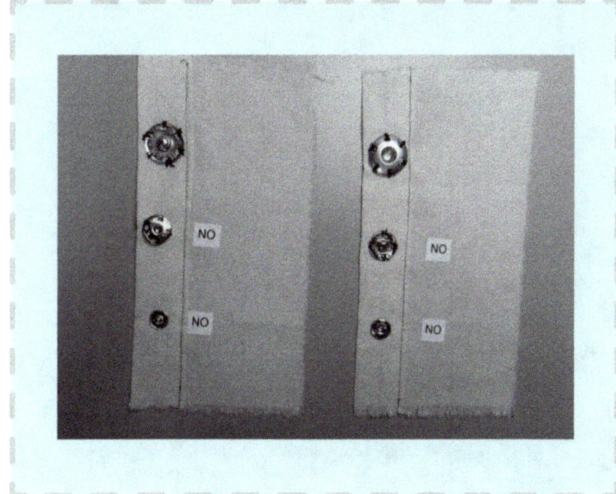


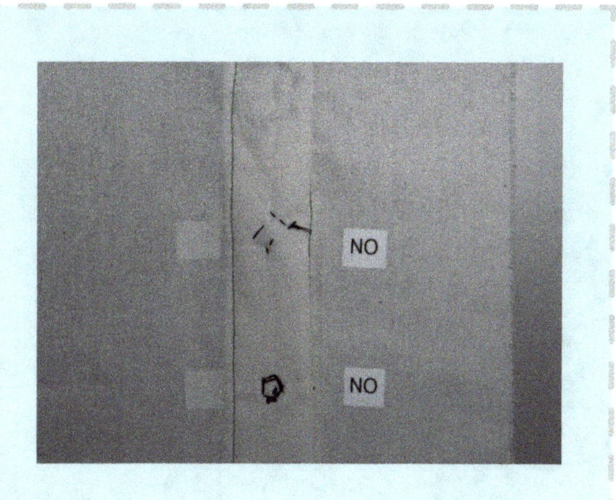

## Hooks and Eyes

1. Use two pieces of fabric, prepared as described in Buttons & Snaps.
2. Double-thread a hand-sewing needle.
3. Prepare two hooks and two eyes.
4. Align fabric for proper closure:
   - » Both hooks and eyes should be attached to the inside of the garment.
   - » When fastened, the two fabric pieces should butt snugly together, not overlap.
5. Sew the hooks:
   - » Attach each hook to the underside of one fabric piece, positioned just inside the folded edge (*not past it*).
   - » Stitch through each hole separately at least 5-7 times.
   - » Secure the shank of the hook by stitching across it—this prevents movement.
6. Sew the eyes:
   - » Attach each eye to the underside of the second fabric piece.
   - » Align them with the hooks, ensuring they do not extend past the fabric edge.
7. Repeat the process for a second hook and eye set, positioned about an inch below the first.

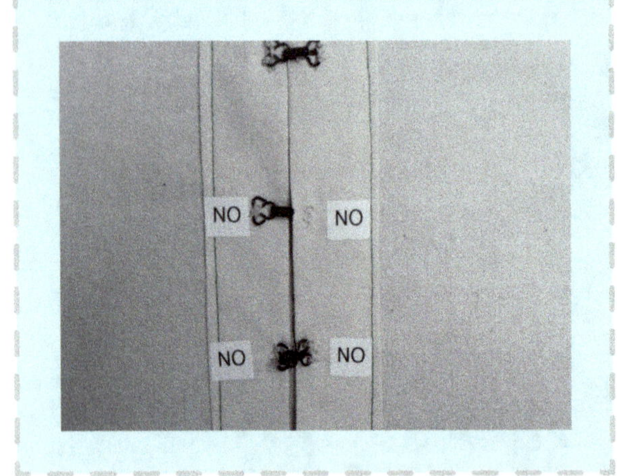


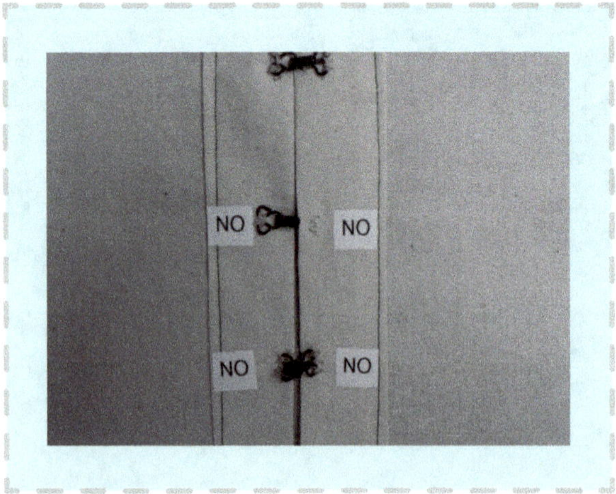

## Bias Facing

Materials Needed:

- One piece of muslin
- One 7" long piece of 1" wide single-fold bias tape
- Pins
- Sewing machine (standard stitch length)
- Hand-sewing needle, single-threaded with Silamide thread
- Iron

 **Instructions:**

1. Open one fold of the bias tape.
   » Think of this fold line as your stitching line.
2. Align the bias tape on the RIGHT side of the fabric, placing the open fold at 5/8" from the edge of the long (7") side.
3. Pin the tape at right angles to the fold/edge.
4. Sew along the fold line using a standard stitch length, backtacking at both ends.
5. Remove the pins and fold the tape to the inside of the fabric along the seam.
6. Press the fold.
7. Pin the free folded edge of the bias tape to the fabric, with pins at right angles to the edge.
8. Hand-stitch the folded edge down using a blind hem stitch with a hand-sewing needle and single-threaded Silamide thread.

Bias facing is used to finish raw edges, particularly curved edges, as an alternative to fabric facings.

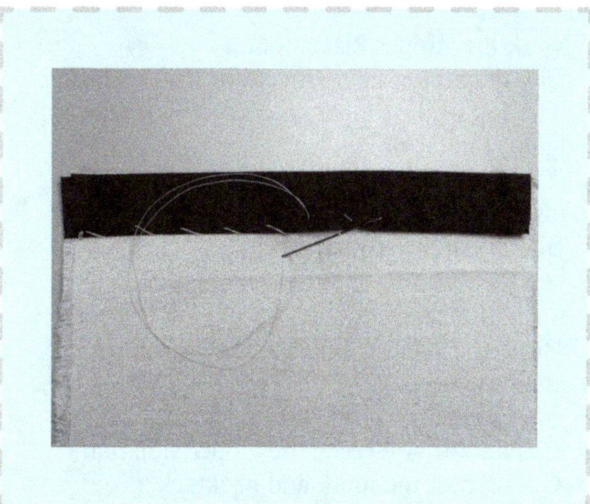

## Centered Zipper

Materials Needed:

- Four pieces of muslin
- One 7" zipper
- Hand-sewing needle, single-threaded with Silamide thread
- Sewing machine with zipper foot attachment
- Tailor's chalk
- Pins
- Iron

 **Instructions:**

Step 1: Prepare the Fabric

1. Sew the short (5") edges of two pieces of fabric together with a flat seam, using a standard stitch length and seam allowance.
   » Backtack at both ends.
2. Press the seam open.
3. Repeat the process with the remaining two pieces of fabric.
4. With RIGHT sides together, pin the two fabric sets together, ensuring:
   » Seam lines match up.
   » Edges remain even.

Step 2: Mark the Zipper Placement

5. Lay the zipper along the seam line, ensuring:
   » The top of the zipper tape aligns with the top edge of the fabric.
   » The fabric is marked where the zipper stop ends. 01 02
6. Set the zipper aside.

Step 3: Baste the Seam

7. Baste the seam together on the machine at 5/8" seam allowance: 03
   » Start at the top (DO NOT backtack).
   » Baste until you reach the zipper stop mark.
   » Go ¼" past the mark and backtack.
   » Switch stitch length back to standard and continue sewing to the bottom edge, backtacking at the end.

Step 4: Insert the Zipper

8. Press the seam open.
9. Position the zipper face down in the seam, ensuring:
   » Zipper teeth are centered in the seam.
   » The top of the zipper tape aligns with the top edge of the fabric.
10. Pin the zipper in place.
11. Hand-baste the zipper to secure it, sewing through all thicknesses (zipper, seam allowance, and fabric).
12. Remove the pins.

Step 5: Machine-Sew the Zipper

13. Attach a zipper foot to your machine.
14. Starting at the top left of the zipper, sew with the seam centered on the zipper tape.
15. When you reach 1/8"-1/4" past the zipper stop:
    » Turn the corner and sew across the bottom of the zipper tape. 04 05
    » Turn the corner again and sew up the other side.
    » Backtack at the start and finish.

Step 6: Final Touches

16. Check the right side of the fabric:
    » The seams should be straight and even.
17. Remove all basting stitches:
    » Hand-basting holding the zipper in place.
    » Machine-basting used to close the seam under the zipper. 06
18. Open and close the zipper tp ensure smooth function. 07

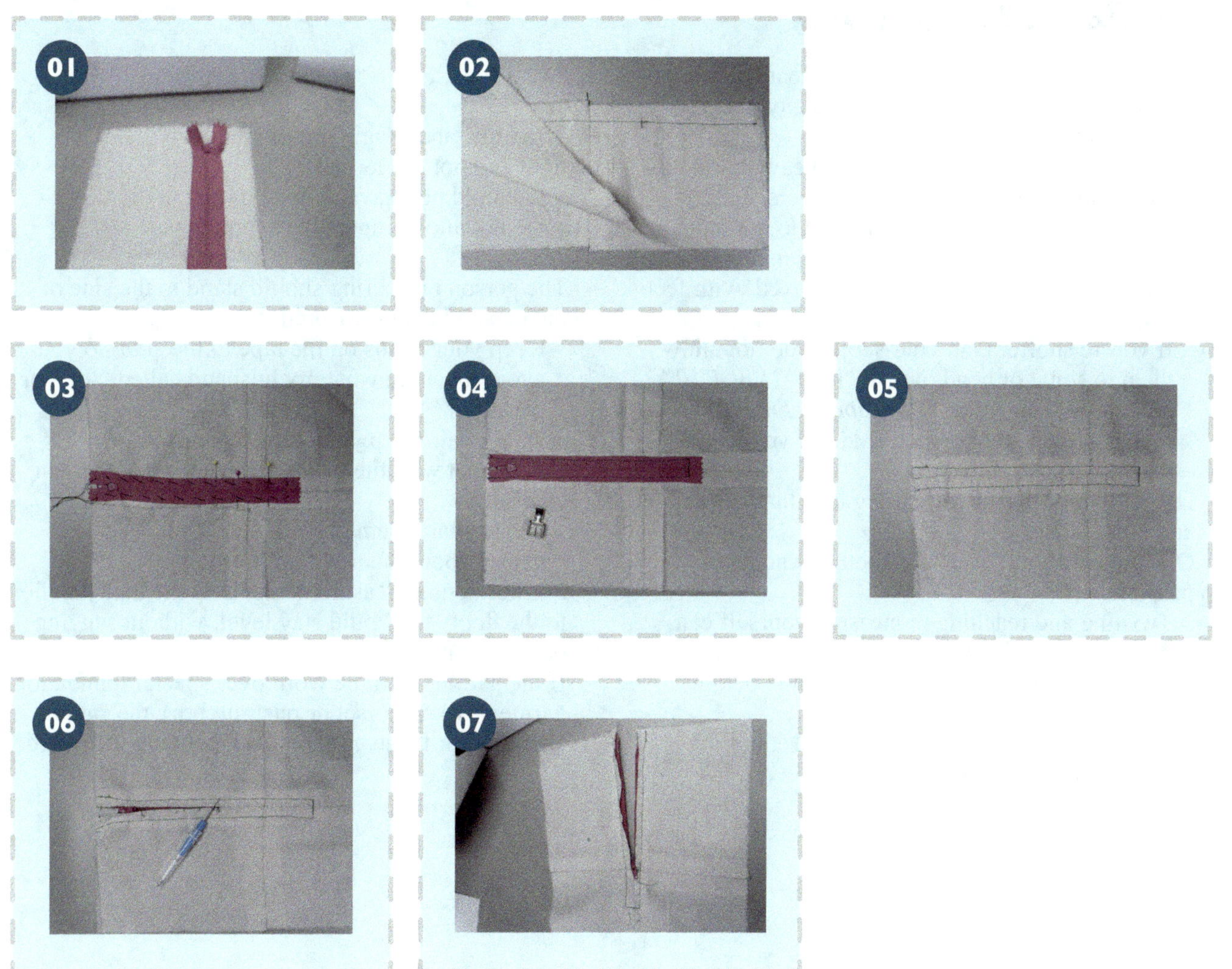
01
02
03
04
05
06
07

# MEASURMENTS

## How to Take Measurements

- The person being measured should wear fitted clothing and remove their shoes and any items from pockets.
  - » Avoid taking measurements over heavy garments like coats, sweaters, or multiple layers.
- Tie a ribbon around the natural waist to maintain a consistent reference point for measurements.
- Have your subject stand erect but relaxed, with feet slightly apart.
  - » If you're shorter than your subject, do not allow them to squat or bend over to "help" (*I'm 4'10" and people always try this—don't let them!*).
  - » Instead, use a stool or step ladder if you can't reach.
- Use a cloth or plastic measuring tape that is flexible and non-elastic.
- One person should measure another whenever possible.
  - » Twisting and reaching to measure yourself can distort the numbers.
- Do not let your subject look down while being measured.
  - » Not because it's a secret, but because looking down distorts the measurements.
- Wrap the tape snugly around the body—not too tight and not too loose.
  - » It should not leave an indentation in the skin.
  - » Do not allow fingers between the tape and the body.
- The person measuring should stand to the side of the person being measured.
  - » Keep your hands on the tape to the side, so you avoid touching what my husband called "the star parts."
  - » Your goal: Keep your subject comfortable.
- Be discreet with the measurements and note them carefully.
  - » Never share them outside the costume shop or gossip about them within the shop.
- For horizontal measurements, hold the tape parallel to the floor—it should stay level, without sagging or drooping.
- If the garment will be worn over special foundation garments (e.g., corset or push-up bra), the subject should wear those garments while being measured.

## Where to Take Measurements

- Bust/Chest – Measure all the way around the chest at the fullest part.
- Waist – Measure where the body bends side to side (*natural waist*).
- Hip – Measure around the fullest part of the hips, typically around the seat.
  - » This is not the high hip area where many pants sit—it is the widest part of the derriere.
- Back Waist Length – Measure from the base of the neck (spine) down to the waistline (*also called Center Back*).
- Neck to Shoulder – Measure from the base of the neck to the shoulder end of the clavicle.
- Center of Shoulder to Bust Point –
  - » The center of the shoulder is where a bra strap typically rests.
  - » The bust point is a polite way of saying "nipple."
  - » If you can't locate the bust point, do not go searching—ask your subject to point it out.
- Bust Point to Bust Point – Measure nipple to nipple.
  - » Again: do not search—ask for help.
- Back Width – Imagine wrapping a towel under your arms.
  - » Measure the straight line from armpit to armpit across the back.

## Measuring for Slopers and Patterns

**Mannequin Measurements**

Use a measuring tape to measure a mannequin as demonstrated in class. These measurements will be used to create your slopers.

- Bust: ____________
- Waist: ____________
- Hip: ____________
- Back Nape to Waist (Center Back): ____________
- Neck to Shoulder: ____________
- Center of Shoulder to Bust Point: ____________
- Bust Point to Bust Point (Front Width): ____________
- Back Width: ____________

**Personal Measurements**

Have a partner measure you. These measurements will help you select a pattern and fabric for your PJ pants.

Important: If your measurements fall under different pattern sizes, choose the largest size and alter it as needed.

» It's easier to take something in than to let it out.

# PATTERN SIZING WARNING

## Patterns lie.

- Do not buy a pattern in the same size as your store-bought clothing.
- Buy patterns based on your measurements, not your usual size.
- Example:
  - » When I buy jeans, I wear a size 6.
  - » If I made my own jeans, I'd need a size 14 pattern.
  - » (*Don't get me started on vanity sizing.*)
- Bust: ____________
- Waist: ____________
- Hip: ____________

# READING A PATTERN ENVELOPE

## Front of Envelope

1. Name of Pattern Company
   - » The most well-known sewing pattern brands are called the "Big 4":
   - » McCall's
   - » Vogue
   - » Butterick
   - » Simplicity
   - » Note: Vogue patterns should not be attempted by beginning sempsters.
2. Pictures of Pattern Options
   - » Illustrations or photos of the different versions of the pattern inside.
   - » Be Aware: Not everything shown on the front is included in the pattern!
3. Pattern Number
   - » Used to locate the pattern in the pattern drawer.
   - » Be Aware: Make sure you select the correct size!

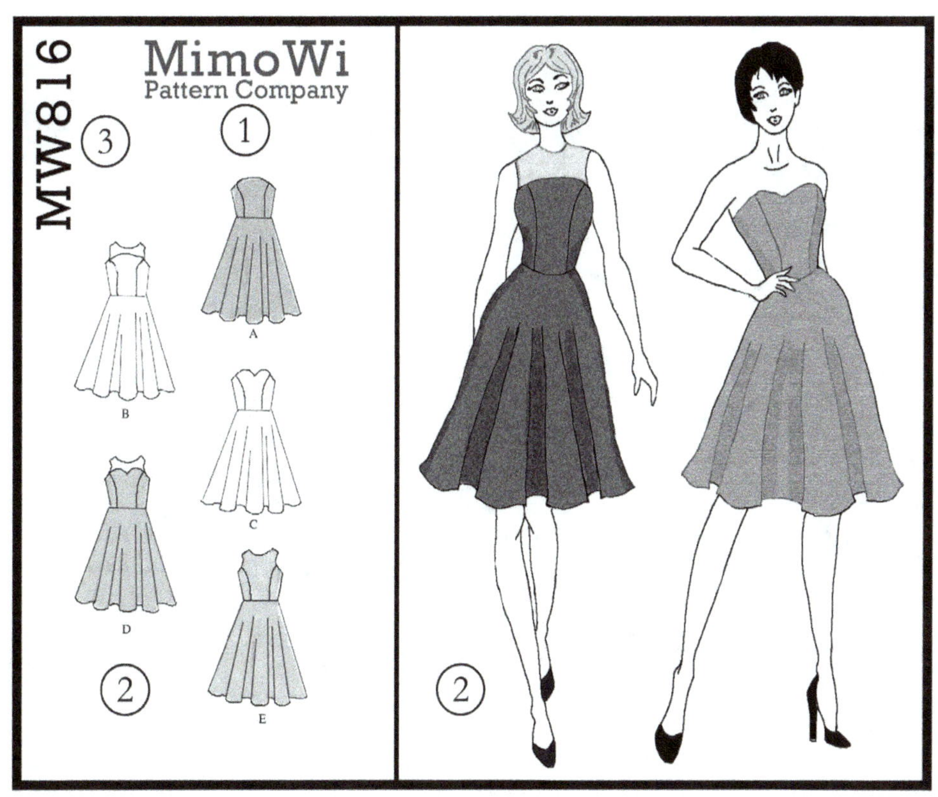

# READING A PATTERN ENVELOPE

## Pattern Envelope Back

(3) **MW816** **MISSES/MISS DRESS WITH BODICE AND SKIRT VARIATIONS** (4)

**15 Pieces**

(8)

| **BODY MEASUREMENTS** | | | | | | | | |
|---|---|---|---|---|---|---|---|---|
| **Bust** | 30 | 31 | 32 | 34 | 36 | 38 | 40 | 42 |
| **Waist** | 23 | 24 | 25 | 26 | 28 | 30 | 32 | 34 |
| **Hip-9" below waist** | 32 | 33 | 34 | 36 | 38 | 40 | 42 | 44 |
| **Back-neck to waist** | 15 | 15.5 | 16 | 16.25 | 16.5 | 17 | 17.25 | 17.5 |

(9)

| **SIZES** | 6 | 8 | 10 | 12 | 14 | 16 | 18 | 20 |
|---|---|---|---|---|---|---|---|---|
| | XS | | S | | M | | L | XL |
| **SIZES - European** | 32 | 34 | 36 | 38 | 40 | 42 | 44 | 46 |

| **A DRESS** | | | | | | | | | Yds |
|---|---|---|---|---|---|---|---|---|---|
| 45" ** | 3 | 3 | 3 | 3 | 3.5 | 3.5 | 3.75 | 4 | |
| 60" ** | 2 | 2 | 2 | 2.5 | 2.5 | 2.5 | 2.5 | 3 | |
| Lining | | | | | | | | | |
| 45" * | 1 | 1.5 | 1.5 | 2.5 | 2.5 | 2.5 | 3 | 3 | |
| **B DRESS** | | | | | | | | | Yds |
| 45" ** cut crosswise | 2.5 | 2.5 | 2.5 | 2.5 | 3 | 3 | 3.5 | 3.5 | |
| 60" ** cut lengthwise | 2 | 2 | 2 | 2 | 2 | 2.5 | 2.5 | 3 | |
| Overdress | | | | | | | | | |
| 45" *** | 3 | 3 | 3 | 3 | 3 | 3 | 3.5 | 4 | |
| 60" *** | 2 | 2 | 2 | 2 | 2 | 2.5 | 2.5 | 3 | |
| Lining | | | | | | | | | |
| 45" * | 2.5 | 1.5 | 2.5 | 2 | 2 | 2.5 | 3 | 3 | |

**Ribbon:** 6-3/4 yd. of 7/8" wide
**Ruffle:** 1-1/8 yd of 54" tulle
**A,B Boning:** 1-7/8 yd of 3/8" wide featherweight

(10) **INTERFACING QUANTITY:** 3/8 yd of 20"-25" of lightweight fusible

(11)

| **GARMENT MEASUREMENTS:** | | | | | | | | |
|---|---|---|---|---|---|---|---|---|
| **A, B Bust:** | 32 | 33 | 34 | 35 | 37 | 40 | 42 | 44 |
| **Finished back length from base of neck:** | 40 | 40 | 41 | 41 | 41 | 41 | 42 | 42 |

(6) **FABRICS:** Silks and silk types, Charmeuse, Crepe Back Satin, Jacquards, Brocade, Satin, Shantung, Taffeta.
Not suitable for stretch fabrics.
Extra fabric needed for plaids, stripes, or one-way designs.

(7) **NOTIONS:** thread, one 14" zipper, hook and eye.
**A:** one ½" button. **B:** Flower

(5) A B

## Back of Envelope

1. Garment/Contents Description
» Describes what the pattern includes (e.g., a blouse in multiple styles, pants and shorts, a vest with ties, etc.).
» Be Aware: Not everything shown on the front is included!
2. Flats (Technical Drawings)
» Computerized illustrations showing important design details like darts, seams, buttons, and zippers.
» Be Aware: Flats reveal how a garment is constructed and may highlight details you didn't notice in the front picture.
3. Fabric Suggestions
» Lists recommended fabric types and fabrics to avoid.
» You don't HAVE to follow them, but your final garment will turn out better if you do.
» Be Aware: Using the wrong fabric will affect fit, drape, and wearability.
4. Notions (Extra Supplies Needed)
» Lists all additional materials needed to complete the project besides fabric and interfacing (e.g., buttons, elastic, zipper, thread).
» Be Aware: Buy your notions with your fabric to ensure they match and so you have everything you need before you start.
5. Body Measurements
» Use your actual body measurements to select the closest size.
» Follow the chart to determine how much fabric you'll need for your size.
» Be Aware: Pattern sizes DO NOT match store clothing sizes!
» If you fall between sizes, or your bust, waist, and hip measurements suggest multiple sizes,
» Go with the largest size and adjust later.
6. Fabric Requirements
» Lists the amount of fabric needed based on your chosen style, size, and fabric width.
» Be Aware:
» Fabric widths vary—45" and 60" are the most common.
» Narrower fabric (45") requires more yardage than wider fabric (60").
» Always double-check before purchasing!
7. Interfacing Quantity
» Interfacing is a stiff material applied to the wrong side of fabric to add structure and support.
» Used in collars, waistbands, cuffs, and buttonholes to prevent sagging.
» Can be fusible (iron-on) or sewn-in.
» Be Aware: Skipping interfacing is a bad idea!
» Necklines will droop, buttonholes will stretch, and your garment won't hold its shape.
» Match the weight and color of interfacing to your fabric for best results.
8. Finished Garment Measurements
» Indicates the amount of extra ease built into the pattern to allow for movement and drape.
» Be Aware:
» If the garment is exactly your body's measurements, you won't be able to move without popping seams or tearing fabric.
9. Fabric With or Without Nap
» Nap means the fabric looks different depending on how it's positioned (e.g., velvet, corduroy, suede).
» Be Aware:
» Fabrics with nap or one-way designs require extra yardage.
» Don't skimp! Cutting fabric incorrectly will ruin the final look.

# A WORD ABOUT INTERFACING

Interfacing is a specialized fabric that adds structure and support to garments.

- Applied to the wrong side of the fabric, it prevents sagging and distortion in areas like:
  - » Collars
  - » Cuffs
  - » Waistbands
  - » Buttonholes

**There are three main types of interfacing:**

1. Fusible (Iron-on) – Bonds to fabric when heated with an iron.
2. Sew-in – Must be stitched in place.
3. Knit – Offers stretch while maintaining structure.

Interfacing usually comes in black or white—match it to your fabric color.

**Is Interfacing Necessary?**

YES. Always use interfacing if the pattern calls for it.

- It adds durability and structure, making your garment look professional.
- Skipping interfacing can ruin the fit and drape—don't take shortcuts!

# PATTERN GUIDE SHEETS (THE INSTRUCTIONS)

Inside your pattern envelope, you will find one or more printed guide sheets. These sheets provide detailed step-by-step instructions for assembling your garment.
Sketches and diagrams are included to help visualize the instructions.

What's on the First Page?

The first page of the guide sheets typically contains:

- Cutting layouts – Shows how to arrange pattern pieces on fabric.
- Explanation of marking symbols – Defines notches, dots, grain lines, and cutting lines.
- General directions – Includes tips for cutting, assembling, and sewing.
- Line drawings of pattern pieces – Each piece is labeled with a letter or number to identify what's needed for each view/style.
- How to lengthen or shorten pattern pieces – Instructions for adjusting pattern proportions.
- Fabric preparation notes – Sometimes includes specific tips for cutting or handling fabric.
- Fabric key – Explains the meaning of shading and symbols on the guide sheet

## Cutting Layouts

- Cutting layouts show how to properly place pattern pieces on fabric to ensure:
  - » The correct fit.
  - » The best fabric usage.
  - » Pattern alignment with grainlines, nap, or one-way designs.
- Layouts may vary by:
  - » View and size.
  - » Fabric width (e.g., 45" vs. 60").
  - » Fabric nap (e.g., velvet, corduroy).
- Tip: I recommend circling the layout for your garment, then:
  - » Circle the pattern pieces needed.
  - » Cross them off as you cut them from the tissue.

# ATTACH PATTERN FLAP & FABRIC SWATCH

# PROJECT PATTERNS

## SPIRAL PRACTICE SHEET

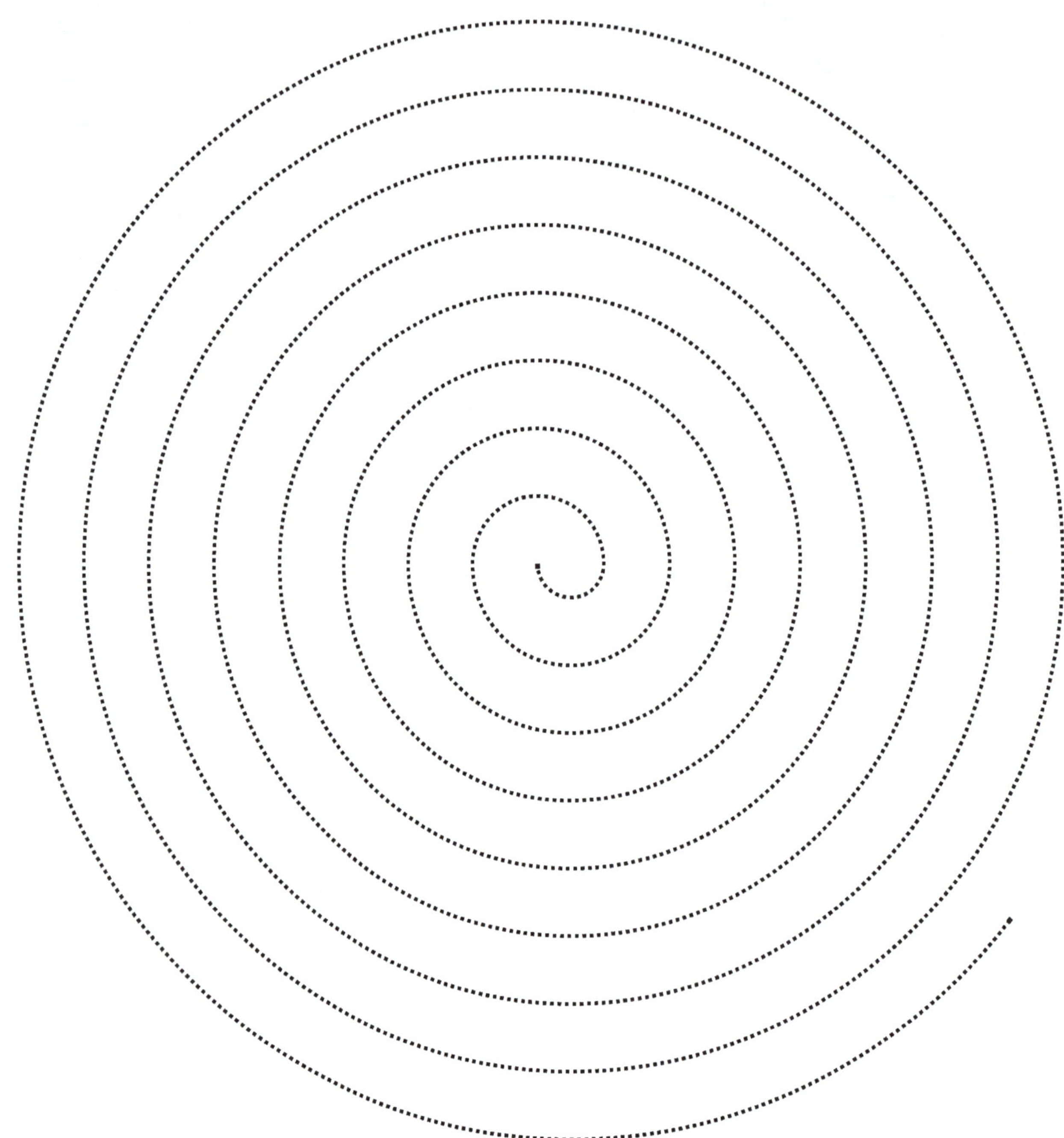

# OUTER CURVE PRACTICE

Cut 2. 5/8" seam allowance included.

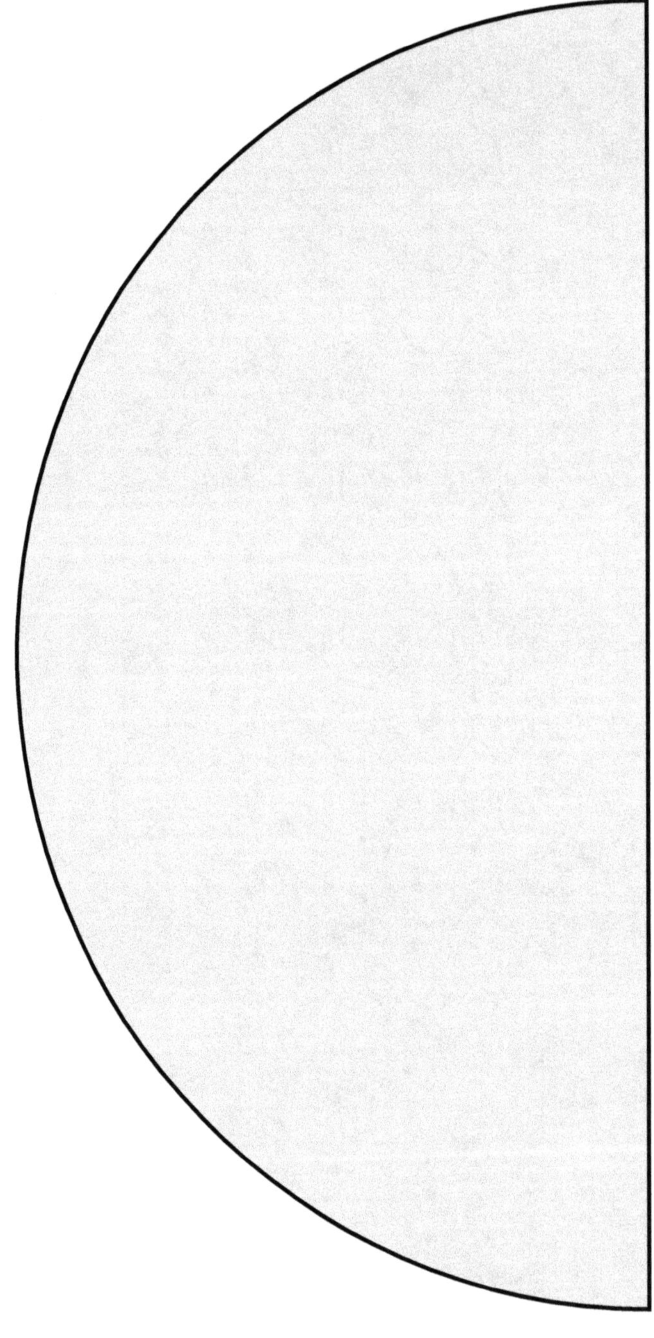

## INNER CURVE

Cut 2. 5/8: seam allowance included.

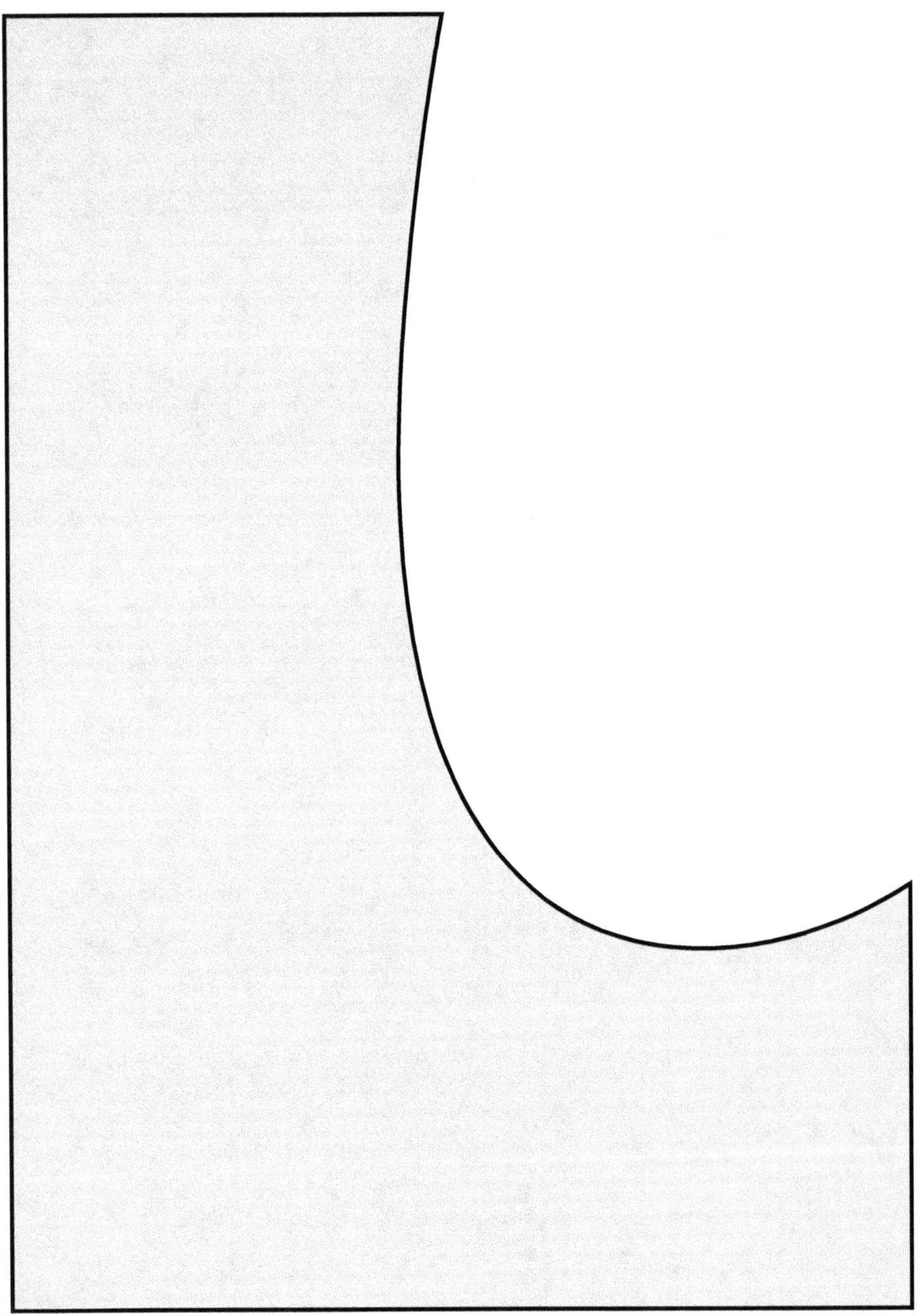

## DART

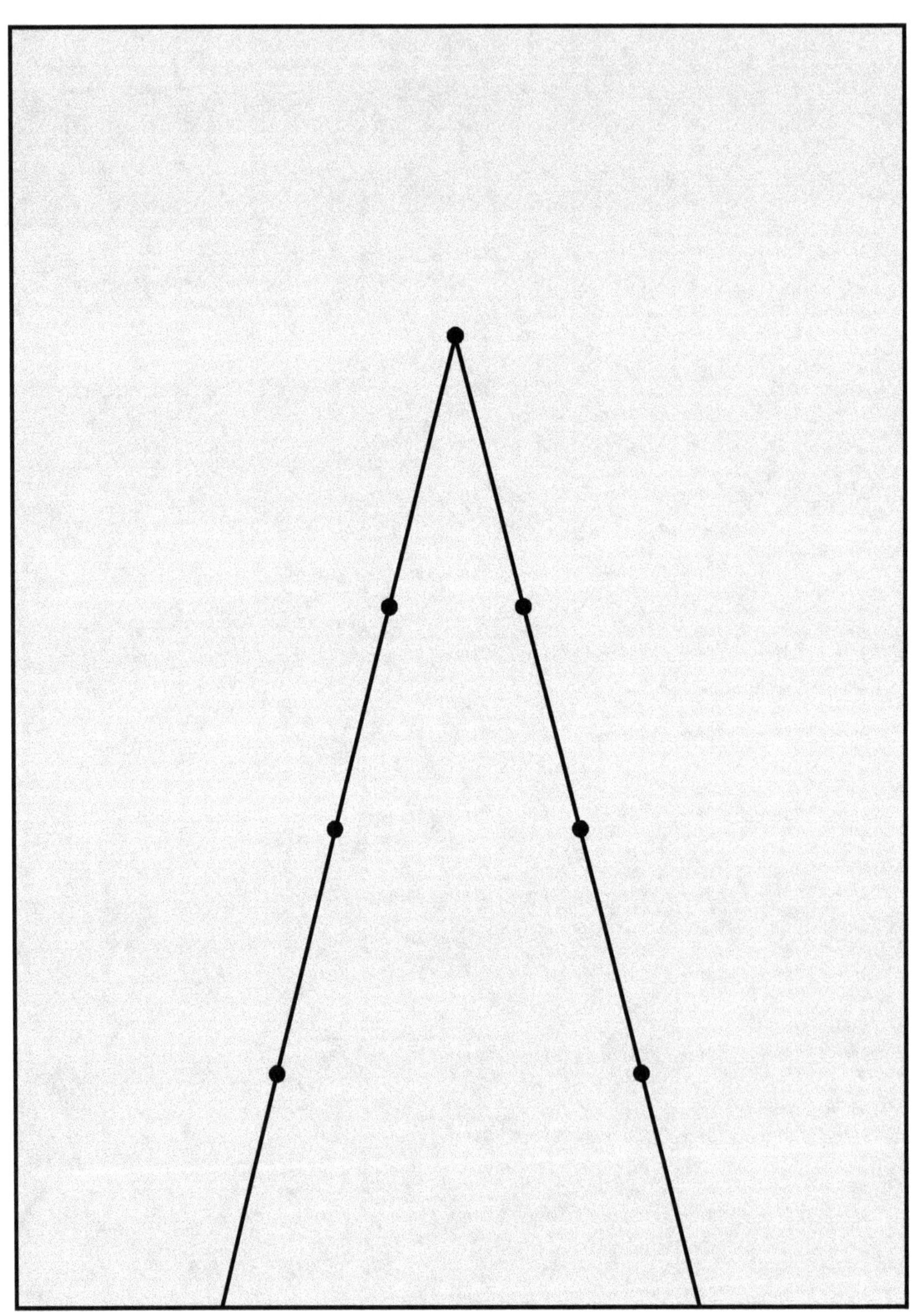

## 2-POINT DART

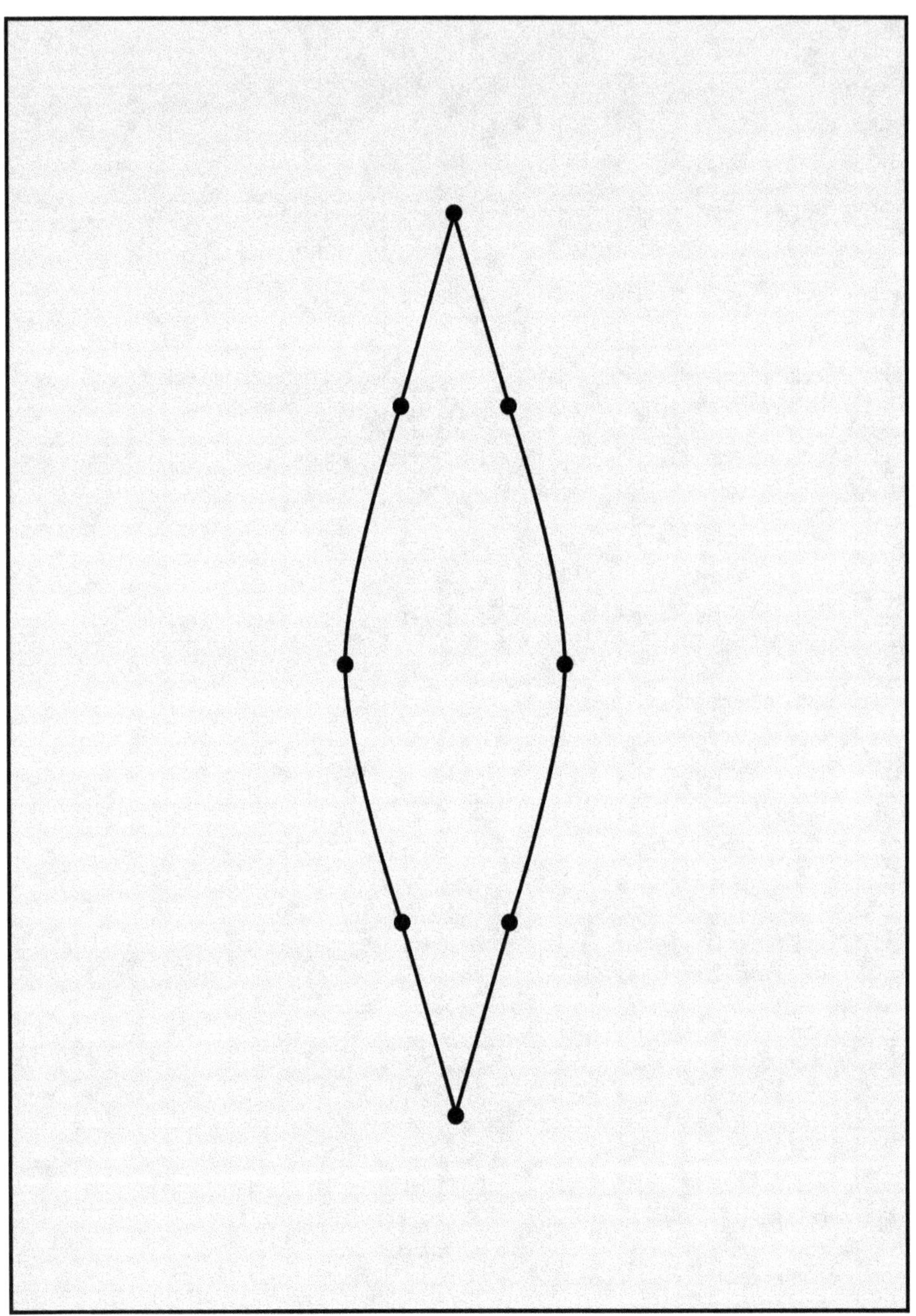

## PRINCESS SEAM

Please Note: sew princess seam with a 1⁄4 “ seam allowance.

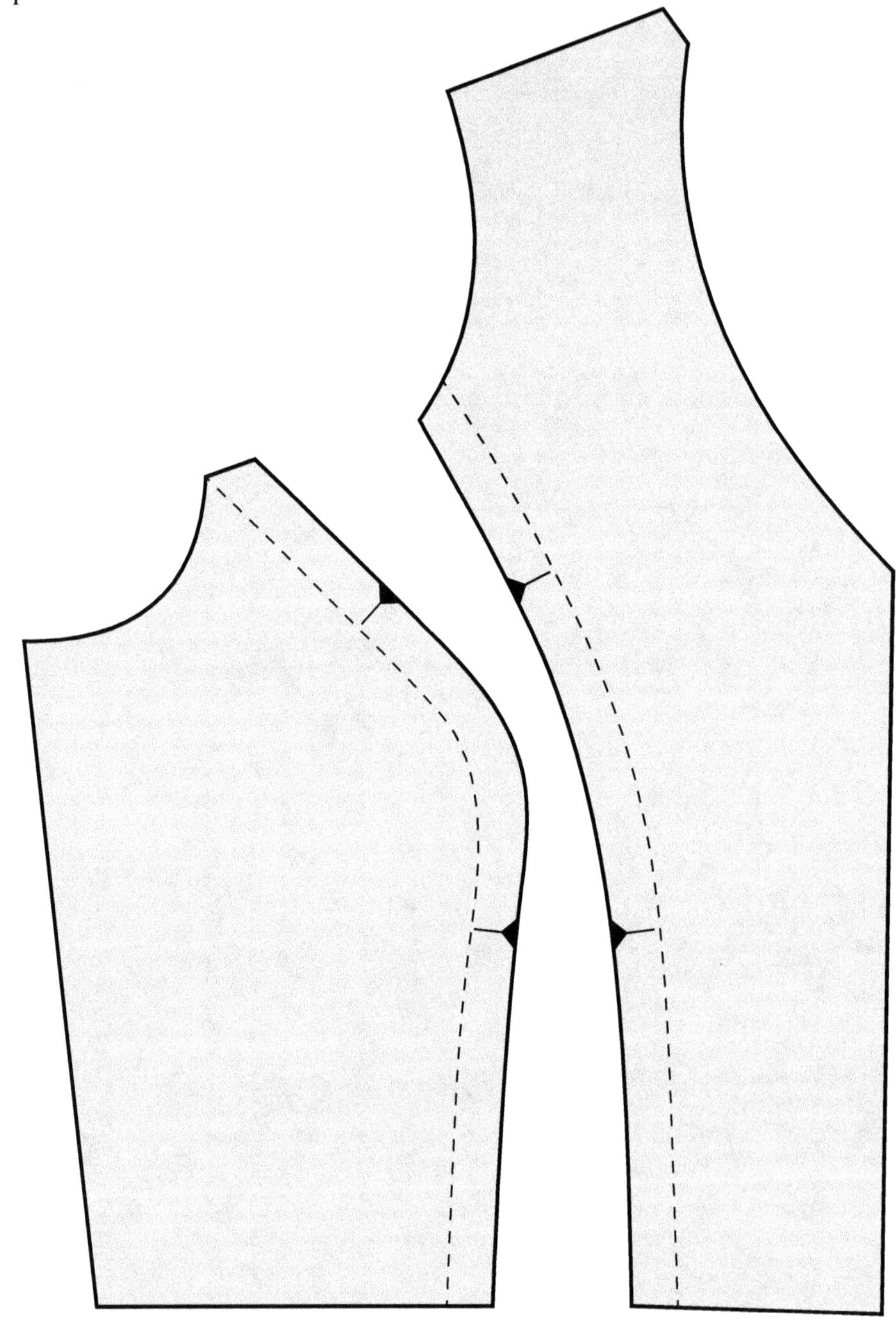

# SEWING MACHINE PARTS & NOTIONS

## Sewing Machine Parts (Will be on the test!)

- Bobbin Winder
- Bobbin
- Spool Pin
- Bobbin Case
- Thread Guide
- Bobbin Compartment
- Thread Take-Up Lever
- Presser Foot
- Needle
- Face Plate
- Feed Dogs
- Stitch Length Regulator
- Stitch Width Regulator
- Hand Wheel
- Foot Pedal

## Exams & Testing

**Midterm Test**

- Identify notions
- Identify sewing machine parts

**Final Exam**

- Identify notions
- Identify sewing machine parts
- Identify pattern symbols
- Thread a sewing machine
- Wind a bobbin

## Notions (Will be on the test!)

- 2-Hole Flat Button
- 4-Hole Flat Button
- Bobbin
- Cone Thread
- C-Thru Ruler
- Double-Threaded Needle
- French Curve
- Hook and Eye
- Iron
- Needle
- Pin
- Pin Cushion
- Point Turner
- Safety Pin
- Scissors/Shears
- Seam Ripper
- Seam Roll
- Sewing Gauge
- Shank Button
- Single-Threaded Needle
- Negative Snap
- Positive Snap
- Spool Thread
- Tailor's Ham
- Tape Measure
- Thimble
- Thread Snips
- Tracing Wheel

# SEWING TERMINOLOGY & TECHNIQUES

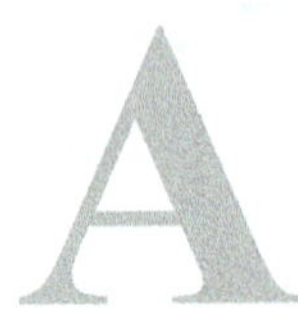

### Anchor Stitch

- Used in hand sewing to secure the thread at the beginning and end of a seam.
- How to do it:
  - » Pull the needle and thread through the fabric until the knot stops you.
  - » Take another stitch in place, going in and out over the knot.
  - » Continue stitching.
  - » When you reach the end of the seam, take another stitch in place before tying the final knot.
  - » Never rely on knots alone to prevent the thread from pulling through the fabric.

## B

### Backtracking

- Also called backstitching.
- Prevents a seam from unraveling by sewing backward over existing stitches at the start and end of a seam.
- How to do it:
  - » Use the reverse function on a sewing machine to sew a few stitches backward, then continue forward.
  - » Think of it as tying a knot with your stitches.

### Baste

- Long, loose stitches used to temporarily hold fabric in place.
- How to do it:
  - » By machine: Set the stitch length to the longest setting.
  - » By hand: Use long, loose stitches.
  - » Do NOT knot the thread or backtack at the beginning or end.
- Uses:
  - » Holding fabric in place before sewing.
  - » Gathering fabric.
  - » Constructing mockups/muslins.

### Bias

- The bias grain is at a 45-degree angle to the straight grain.
- Bias-cut fabric is more elastic and fluid than fabric cut along the straight or cross grain.
- Uses:
  - » Creating drapey, clingy garments.
  - » Adding stretch and movement to designs.

### Bias Tape

- A narrow strip of fabric cut on the bias (at a 45-degree angle to the grain).
- Why use bias tape?
  - » Stretchy and easier to curve than straight-cut fabric.
  - » Used for binding curved edges (***e.g., necklines, armholes, and blanket edges.***)

### Blind Hem Stitch

- A nearly invisible hem used to finish the edge of a garment.
- By hand: Truly invisible from the right side.
- By machine: Leaves small, nearly invisible stitches on the right side (***especially if the thread matches the fabric).***

### Bobbin

- A small spool that feeds the bottom thread in a sewing machine.
- A machine cannot sew without a bobbin.

### Body

- Refers to a fabric's firmness, texture, and ability to retain shape.

# C

### Casing

- A folded-over fabric channel used to hold:
  - » Elastic
  - » A drawstring
  - » Other inserts

### Chalk

- Used for marking fabric to indicate pleats, darts, buttonholes, or cutting lines.
- NEVER use pens, pencils, or markers on fabric!
- Types of fabric markers:
  - » Chalk (pencils, sticks, tiles, wheels)
  - » Disappearing ink markers
  - » Wax marking tools
- ALWAYS test first to make sure the marking will disappear from your fabric.

### Clip / Clip the Curves

- Used to flatten a curved seam by snipping the seam allowance at regular intervals.
- How to do it:
  - » Snip perpendicular to the seam.
  - » Do NOT cut into the stitch line!

### Cross Grain

- The grain of the fabric that runs in the direction of the weft threads, perpendicular to the selvage edges.

### Crossways Fold

- Instead of folding fabric lengthwise (selvage to selvage), the fabric is folded cut edge to cut edge to accomodate wider pattern pieces.

### Cutting Line

- Found on paper patterns, this dark line is marked with the size.
- Modern patterns often include multiple sizes on each piece be sure to follow the line for your correct size.

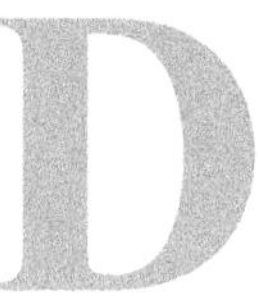

### Dart

- A fold and stitch technique used to shape garments.
- Common dart locations:
  - » Bust and waist.
- Darts vary in width, lenght, and may taper at one or both ends.

### Drape

- Refers to how fabric hangs on the body or dress form.

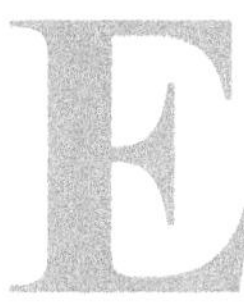

### Ease

- Extra space in a seam to allow movement.
- How to works:
  - » One garment edge is slightly longer than the matching edge.
  - » The shorter edge is stretched slightly to match.
- Purpose:
  - » Prevents fabric from pulling or breaking during movement.

### Ease Stitch

- A longer-than-usual row of stitches, sewn just within the seam allowance.
- Purpose:
  - » Allows fabric to be sewn onto a smaller piece without puckering or gathering.

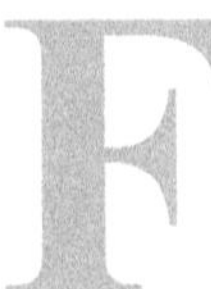

### Facing

- Fabric used to finish raw edges of a garment, usually at necklines and armholes.
- Types:
  - » Shaped facings - Cut to match the edge they will finish.
  - » Bias facings - Made from bias tape.

### Feed Dogs

- The "teeth" under the presser foot on the sewing machine.
- Function:
  - » Moves the fabric as it is sewn.
  - » Fabric is fed from front to back, unless sewing in reverse.

### Fold Line

- Indicates a pattern piece should be placed on the fabric fold, so that two identical halves are cut as one.
- Purpose:
  - » Eliminiates center seams.

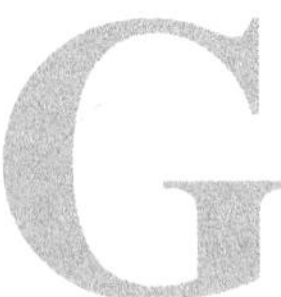

### Gathering

- A technique used to shorten a fabric strip, so a longer piece can be attached.
- Common in:
  - » Clothing to add fullnes.
  - » Decorative details.
- Multiple rows of gathering are called "shirring".

### Grain

- Refers to the direction of warp and weft threads in woven fabric.
  - » Warp threads (vertical/up & down).
  - » Weft threads (horizontal/right to left). (***Tip: Ryhme "weft" with "left" to remember***!)
- Warp-threads are stonger and less likely to stretch..
- Non-woven materials (felt, leather, interfacing) do not have a grain.

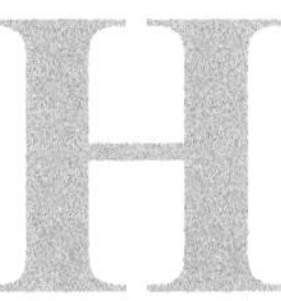

### Hand

- A term used to describe the texture, feel, and weight of a fabric.

### Hand Wheel

- Located on the right side of the sewing machine.
- Function:
  - » Manually moves the needle and feed dogs.
  - » ALWAYS turn counterclockwise (toward you) to prevent jamming.

### Hem

- Definition:
  - » The folded edge of a garment, stitched to create a finished edge.
  - » The process of hemming fabric.

# I

**Interfacing**

- A stabilizing fabric sewn or fused inside a garment to provide structure.
- Uses:
  - » Collars, cuffs, buttons bands, necklines.
- Types:
  - » A Fusible (iron-on).
  - » Sew-in
- Reduces sagging and maintains shape.

# K

**Knit Fabric**

- Created by looping yarn continuously, giving the fabric stretch..
- Common in:
  - » T-shirts, dancewear, undergarment.
- Unravels, but does not fray.

# L

**Lining**

- A layer of fabric inside a garment.
- Purpose:
  - » Adds body to the outer
  - » Prevents sheer fabrics from being see-through.
  - » Helps garments slide over other clothing smoothly.
- Examples:
  - » Lined skirts prevent fabric from clinging to legs.
  - » Lined jackets prevent bunching over shirts.

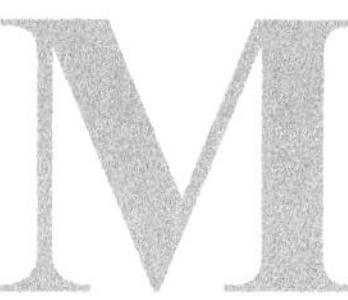

**Mockup (Muslin or Toile)**

- A test version of a garment made from muslin or inexpensive fabric.
- Purpose:
  - » O Checks fit, pattern accuracy, and design before cutting into expensive fabric.

**Muslin**

- A cheap woven fabric often used for:
  - » Crafts
  - » Quilt backings.
  - » Mockups of garments (practice pieces).

# N

### Nap

- Refers to the direction of a fabric pile.
- How to tell:
  - » Brush the fabric with your hand. If it changes color or texture, it has nap.
- Examples:
  - » Velvet, corduroy, suede.
- Important:
  - » All pattern pieces must be in the same direction to avoid mismatched shading.
  - » Nap may requie extra fabric.

### Notch

- Trinagle-shaped markings on the cutting line of a pattern.
- Purpose:
  - » Helps align fabric pieces during sewing.
  - » Match notches together correctly for accurate construction.

### Notions

- All supplies needed for a sewing project (besides fabric).
- Examples:
  - » Zippers, buttons, threads, bias tape, interfacing, elastic.
  - » Tools like seam rippers, pins, scissors, and chalk.

# P

### Pile

- A raised surface on fabric created by extra yarn loops.
- Examples:
  - » Velvet, terry cloth, corduroy.
- Gives fabric a soft, plush texture.

### Pinking Shears

- Scissors with a zig-zag edge.
- Purpose:
  - » Prevents fabric from unraveling by finishing raw edges.

### Pins

- Used to hold patterns in place while cutting and secure fabric layers while sewing.
- Best practice:
  - » Use thin pins to avoid leaving holes in the fabric.
  - » Discard any bent, nicked, or dull pins to prevent fabric damage.

### Point Turner

- A tool with a pointed end used to push out sharp corners and points in fabric.
- Commonly used for:
  - » Collars
  - » Cuffs
  - » Corners of seams

### Press

- Pressing = lifting the iron up and down, not sliding it back and forth.
- Purpose:
  - » Prevents fabric distortion.
  - » Creates crisp seams and pleats.
- Press every seam before moving on to the next construction step.

**Presser Foot**

- A sewing machine attachment that applies downward pressure to hold fabric against the feed dogs, helping it move smoothly.
- Important:
  - » ALWAYS lower the presser foot before sewing.
  - » This engages the tension disks, ensuring even stitches.

**Presser Foot Lever**

- Used to raise and lower the presser foot.
- Location: Usually at the back left of the machine, opposite the presser foot.

**Prewash (Preshrinking)**

- Washing fabric before sewing to prevent shrinkage and color bleeding.
- Wash the fabric the same way it will be cleaned after the garment is made.
- Why?
  - » Prevents finished garments from shrinking after construction.
  - » Ensures dye stability in the fabric.

**Princess Seam**

- A shaping seam that joins two different curved edges to contour the garment.
- Commonly found at:
  - » Bust
  - » Waist
  - » Hips

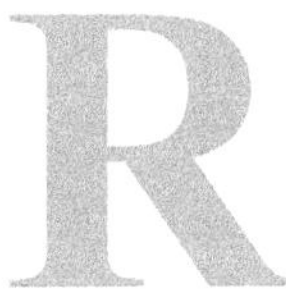

**Raw Edge**

- The cut edge of fabric that is unfinished and prone to fraying.
- Should be finished to prevent raveling.

**Right Side of Fabric**

- "Right" = "Correct" – this is the side meant to show on the finished garment.
- Usually the more decorative, printed, or textured side.

**Right Sides Together (RST)**

- Placing two fabric pieces together so their "right" (correct) sides touch.
- The wrong sides face outward.
- Why?
  - » Ensures the finished seam is hidden on the inside.

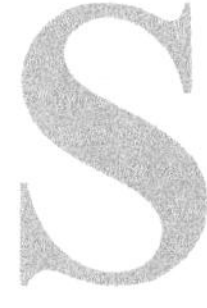

**Seam**

- A line of stitches that joins two or more fabric pieces.
- Types of seams:
  - » Flat seam
  - » French seam
  - » Zigzag seam
  - » Princess seam

**Seam Allowance**

- The space between the fabric edge and the seam line.
- Standard seam allowances:
  - » 5/8" – Most commercial patterns (U.S.)
  - » 1/4" – Common for quilting
  - » 1" or more – Costumes (allows for future alterations)
- Always follow the seam allowance listed in the pattern instructions to avoid incorrect sizing.

**Seam Ripper**

- A small, sharp tool used to remove stitches when mistakes happen.
- How to use it:
  - » Insert the sharp point under a stitch.
  - » Use the tiny blade to cut the thread.
  - » Repeat as needed to remove the entire seam.
- A stitcher's best friend!

**Selvage**

- The woven edge of fabric that prevents fraying and unraveling.
- Runs the length of the fabric.
- Often has manufacturer/designer information printed on it.

**Sloper (Also called a *Body Block* or *Master Pattern*)**

- A base pattern used to develop other patterns.
- Highly accurate and designed to fit specific measurements.
- Used as a foundation for creating stylized garment designs.

**Snap**

- A fastening device with two parts:
  - » Negative (innie) snap – fits into the positive.
  - » Positive (outie) snap – holds the negative snap in place.
- Attachment Methods:
  - » Sewn-in by hand.
  - » Pronged snaps attached with a special snap tool (similar to pliers).
- Available in a variety of sizes.

**Staystitch**

- A single row of straight stitches sewn through one layer of fabric.
- Purpose:
  - » Prevents stretching on curves.
  - » Stabilizes fabric before it is sewn into a seam.
- Uses a slightly smaller stitch length than regular stitching.

**Stitch in the Ditch**

- A method of stitching facings or bias binding to the underside of fabric.
- How to do it:
  - » Stitch on the right side of the fabric, inside the seam (in the "ditch").
  - » Pull the seam open slightly while stitching so the thread stays hidden.

**Stitch Length**

- Refers to the size of each stitch.
- Common stitch lengths:
  - » 11-12 stitches per inch – Regular sewing.
  - » 6 stitches per inch – Basting, gathering, sleeve easing.
  - » Rarely exceeds 12 per inch, except for fine detailing.

**Stitching Line**

- Depicted as a thin, broken line on patterns.
- Indicates the seam line where fabric pieces should be stitched together.

**Straight Grain**

- Runs in the direction of the warp threads (parallel to the selvage).
- The strongest grainline with minimal stretch.
- Why does it matter?
  - » Most garments are cut with the straight grain running top to bottom.
  - » If the grainline is ignored, the garment may twist or hang unevenly.
- Pattern symbols:
  - » The long arrow on a pattern corresponds to the fabric's grainline.

**Swatch**

- A small fabric sample used for:
  - » Testing fabric appearance and texture.
  - » Matching fabric colors and types without carrying large fabric pieces.
- Fabric stores may offer swatches for free or for a small fee.

# T

### Tack

- A temporary stitch used to hold fabric pieces together before final sewing.
- Usually removed after final stitching.

### Tailor's Ham (Also called a *Dressmaker's Ham* or *Pressing Ham*)

- A ham-shaped stuffed cushion used for pressing curved areas.
- Commonly used for:
  - » Darts
  - » Sleeves
  - » Princess seams

### Tape Measure

- A long, flexible measuring tape used for taking body and fabric measurements.
- Usually yellow, with inches on one side and centimeters on the other.

### Tension

- Refers to the balance between the upper and lower (bobbin) threads.
- Correct tension ensures:
  - » Flat, even stitches with no puckers.
  - » Strong, durable seams that do not break or bunch.
- If tension is off:
  - » Threads may snarl or jam.
  - » Seams may become too weak (easily popped) or too tight (causing puckering).

### Thread

- A thin strand of fiber (cotton, nylon, polyester, silk, etc.) used for sewing.
- Not rope, string, or yarn—just thread!
- Different weights for different uses – always use the correct type for your project.

### Thread Cutter

- A built-in feature on some sewing machines for cutting thread ends.
- Location:
  - » Near the machine needle or on the side of the machine.
- To use:
  - » Slide the thread along the blade to cut.

### Topstitch

- A decorative or functional stitch sewn near a seam.
- Uses:
  - » Holds fabric in place.
  - » Strengthens edges and hems.
  - » Adds a decorative finish.
- Unlike regular stitching, topstitching does not join fabric pieces together.

### Tracing Paper

- Special paper with ink, chalk, or wax on one side.
- Used with a tracing wheel to mark fabric for cutting and sewing.

### Tracing Wheel

- A small, spiked wheel (like a pizza cutter) used to transfer pattern markings to fabric.
- How to use:
  - » Place tracing paper (ink side down) on the fabric.
  - » Place the pattern piece on top of the tracing paper.
  - » Roll the tracing wheel over the markings to transfer them to the fabric.
- Important:
  - » Do not press too hard – you may cut the fabric or paper.
  - » Always mark the wrong side of the fabric.
  - » Test tracing paper first – some marks do not wash out easily.

### Turn

- Flipping fabric right-side out after sewing.
- Typically done after sewing fabric pieces together with right sides facing.

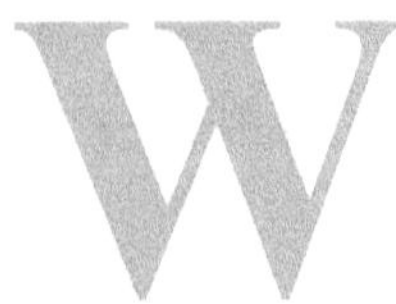

## W

**Woven Fabric**

- Created by weaving yarns at right angles (warp & weft).
- Stretch properties:
  - » No stretch lengthwise (warp).
  - » Minimal stretch crosswise (weft).
  - » Some stretch along the bias (diagonal).
- Edges fray and should be finished to prevent unraveling.

**Wrong Side (of the Fabric)**

- The "inside" or less decorative side of fabric.
- How to identify:
  - » Some fabrics look identical on both sides.
  - » Others have a clear right and wrong side – the wrong side is usually duller or plainer.

**Wrong Sides Together (WST)**

- When two fabric pieces are placed with their wrong sides touching before sewing.
- Used for:
  - » French seams.
  - » Exposed edge finishes.

## Y

**Yardage**

- Refers to the length of fabric needed for a sewing project.
- Patterns specify yardage based on:
  - » Garment size.
  - » Fabric width (45" vs. 60").
  - » Fabric type (nap vs. no nap).

## Z

**Zigzag Stitch**

- A wide stitch that moves back and forth in a zigzag pattern.
- Uses:
  - » Sewing stretchy fabrics.
  - » Finishing raw edges.
  - » Reinforcing buttonholes.

# SUPPLIES REQUIRED

- Fabric & Notions:
  - 3 yards muslin
  - 3 yards pajama pant fabric
  - Elastic
  - Thread (*Waxed Silamide for hand sewing, or spool thread for both hand and machine sewing*)
  - 2-hole button
  - 4-hole button
  - Shank button
  - Hook and eye closure
  - Sew-on snaps

- Tools & Equipment:
  - Sewing shears
  - Sewing needles
  - Sewing pins
  - Tailor's chalk, Frixion pens, or disappearing marker
  - Iron and ironing board
  - Seam ripper
  - Seam gauge
  - Tape measure
  - Tracing paper and tracing wheel
  - Craft paper
  - C-thru ruler
  - Right angle ruler
  - Commercial pajama pant pattern

## Recommended Books

For further learning, these books are highly recommended:

- *The Costume Technician's Handbook* – Rosemary Ingham & Liz Covey
- *Costume Construction* – Katherine Strand-Evans
- *Sewing Machine Magic* – Stephanie Lincecum
- *Reader's Digest Complete Guide to Sewing*

# About the Author

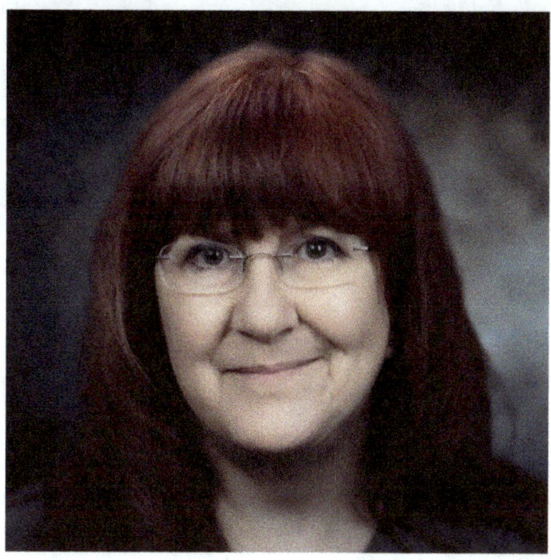

Michelle Elliot Winchester was taught to sew at the age of nine and made her first costume in fifth grade. Her interest in theatre began in high school, where she was assigned to the costume shop—and never looked back.

Misha has costumed productions for high school theatre, community theatre, university theatre, and summer stock. During her undergraduate studies at Minot State University, she ran the university costume shop, learning alongside her classmates and friends.

Determined to expand her knowledge, she pursued an MFA in Costume Design and Technology at the University of South Dakota. It was during graduate school that she discovered her true passion—teaching others what she had learned.

For the past 20 years, Misha has taught a wide range of subjects at the university level, including:

- Costume Design
- Costume Construction
- Stage Makeup
- Rendering for the Stage
- Fashion History
- Script Analysis
- Stage Management
- Introduction to Theatre

Outside of theatre, she is a devoted mother and grandmother. She is blessed with an unbelievably supportive son and daughter, an incredibly easy-going son-in-law, and the smartest granddaughter ever born.

Michelle is also owned by six cats—Rosencrantz, Guildenstern, Polonius, Horatio, Coriolanus, and Ophelia.

www.ingramcontent.com/pod-product-compliance
Lightning Source LLC
La Vergne TN
LVHW080248110826
845148LV00023BA/866

* 9 7 9 8 8 9 4 4 1 0 2 6 5 *